EAT **HAPPY**

Transform Your Health with Foods You Love

ALISSA GLENN

Kevin and Mary,
I hope you enjoy
the book and Eat Happy!

Alissa Glenn

This book is dedicated to my endlessly supportive husband Jacob,
my kids who are my constant source of drive and inspiration,
and my parents who taught me everything I know
about food made with love.

TABLE OF CONTENTS

FOREWARD

8/15/2014

It's 4pm and I'm madly rushing to finish chapters on the manuscript of my first book, which I'm so excited about. If I get it done in the next week I'll have an awesome opportunity to present and advertise my book at the Institute for Integrative Nutrition Conference in November, attended by 10,000 people! So exciting, so cool. I have to do this.

My 2 year old and 4 year old are screaming at each other downstairs, my sitter is off in an hour, and I'm 38 weeks pregnant, uncomfortable, grumpy, and rather stressed. Dinner time looms. I have Eat Happy Meal Plans that I need to write and schedule in advance over the next few weeks so I can take a mini-break when the baby comes. The baby room isn't set up, no bags have been packed, and I'm banking too much on the fact that my other two kids were nearly two weeks late. I need more time to get everything done.

I have wanted to order pizza for the kids for dinner, pretty much every night for the last few weeks, and tonight is no exception. The leftovers are gone and I've exhausted my go-to quick and healthy dinner ideas. They'd love the pizza obviously. But it's not going to do them any favors (they're just getting over a summer time cold), it won't really do me any favors, as it's not exactly a go-to food to enhance my productivity (quite the opposite). My book, Eat Happy: Transform Your Health with Foods You Love, is all about how to easily transition to real food.

I get how hard it can be to work up the motivation to put real food on the table. I meander around the kitchen and pantry for a while, taking into account what is available and can be made quickly into some semblance of a meal, all the while thinking that I can fall back on the pizza. The kids aren't completely attacking each other, which is helpful.

Ultimately I'm persuaded by all of the farmer's market produce still hanging out in my fridge; it's the end of the week and it needs to be eaten. Snap peas, fresh corn, and some cute sweet peppers called "sweeties" that everyone loves don't require much prep or cooking time. I have some purple rice that cooks in 30 minutes, and some fully cooked and frozen black-eyes peas that can thaw in the sauté pan.

A few cloves of garlic, juice from a lemon, some salt and pepper. It's all that I feel like mustering up. The kids pick some basil from the garden (the 2 year old slams the door on the 4 year old in the process, resulting in some screaming, but they still seem to have fun with it). Dinner is ready in 30 minutes. In retrospect it wasn't much harder than going to pick up pizza would be.

It's a small victory. That doesn't mean pizza never happens. For tonight, anyways, we all get some very fresh and rather beautiful food. Even better, there are leftovers for lunch.

~ *Alissa*

INTRODUCTION

Eat Happy

Let's get one thing straight: I love food. I love nothing more than a leisurely dinner with friends and family with heart-warming dishes, or a picnic on the grass with a deliciously loaded picnic basket. I agree with the idea that food is love. Some of my most cherished memories have been around a table.

Yet we live in a culture that encourages and provokes all kinds of negative emotions around food. Most people are not blissfully enjoying their meals. Quite the opposite - they're wracked with guilt, anger, frustration, and confusion. I fell into this pit myself when I was in my early twenties. A lot of stress and frustration from other areas of my life embedded into my eating habits. I worried about calories, fat grams, and gaining weight. It sucked, and it certainly didn't help make me any healthier or happier.

I want you to know the experience of eating and the physical and emotional results do not have to be drenched in these negative emotions. Food can and should be a positive experience all around. One of the best things I ever did was to take a teaching assistant position in France when I was twenty five years old. Completely absent was the anxiety and stress around eating, and the pressure constantly glaring at me from newsstands and TV commercials to be neurotic about food and weight. Suddenly I was immersed in a culture that loves and reveres its food. Those eight months were more than refreshing; they were healing. I learned the less you worry about food, the better off you'll be.

I love to pass this love for food on to my clients, and to teach them how to eat in a way that makes their bodies feel vibrant and that leaves them emotionally fulfilled, spiritually connected, and satisfied.

It is possible, and it's so much easier than you think.

In this book I want to share with you the single most important dietary change that you can make in order to Eat Happy. It isn't a strict diet, doesn't require you to live like a caveman, nor does it involve expensive ingredients or supplements.

It's a simple rule: <u>transition your diet to unprocessed foods, i.e. "real food"</u>. This incredibly powerful change will transform your health, your life, and likely many of the lives around you. While this shift is simple, it is something that took me years to understand and fully wrap my mind around.

Most people don't realize they're eating large quantities of processed food. I certainly didn't. Due to the nature of our food supply and the way our culture of eating has evolved, it's become ingrained in nearly all of our typical daily foods. Even our "fresh-baked" or "home-made" food products are made from highly processed ingredients.

Transitioning to an unprocessed diet takes awareness and some simple tools. This is what I'm so excited to communicate to you in this book, as well as the amazing benefits of making this change.

This book will give you everything you need to know to get started. First I'll talk about how powerful and incredible unprocessed foods are at transforming health; food truly is medicine. Then I'll discuss processed foods: what they are, where they're found, why they're problematic, and how they reduce physical and emotional health.

Then it gets even more fun. I'll talk about the incredible world of unprocessed foods. There are so many delicious foods to try, and they're easy to prepare! In the chapter What to Eat, I'll introduce these foods. <u>Nearly every processed food has an unprocessed equivalent that has more nutrition and better flavor</u>. The rest of the book is dedicated to providing practical preparation and cooking tips, which even a cooking novice will find approachable and can quickly master.

When I started my journey with food ten years ago, I thought I knew a lot. It's taken ten years to get the perspective that I now hope to give to you. With it I know that, like me, you can Eat Happy.

My Story

When I was twenty-four years old, I was healthy, technically speaking. I exercised regularly, ate the recommended carb-heavy, low-fat diet, and generally took good care of myself. But I did not feel good or healthy most of the time, and I had the prescriptions to prove it.

I had chronic digestive problems, diagnosed as IBS, regular migraine headaches and sinus infections, acid reflux paired with acute burning stomach pain, and horrible seasonal allergies. To treat these issues at any given time I was taking four to six prescription medications.

At the same time I had developed a dysfunctional attitude towards food. I rarely felt satisfied, craved sugar constantly, and felt that at some point along the way I had lost control of my ability to self-regulate. I scrutinized food and counted calories - a practice I now detest.

At some point I looked at my drawer of drugs and thought: "This is crazy". I could not reconcile that I should need that many medications, or that the symptoms I was experiencing were unavoidable. It just didn't make sense. More importantly, I worried these symptoms were the surface reflections of more concerning underlying issues; I didn't want to let anything fester that could turn into serious conditions down the road. I decided that I needed to be more proactive at figuring these things out. At the time I was working as a research analyst in Washington D.C., and my analytical background in economics, math and statistics made me inclined to look for concrete solutions to these problems.

It took a long time. I started reading about the health benefits of various foods. I slowly cut down on and eventually eliminated prescription medications. I read about different dietary approaches. Ultimately I decided to more formally study holistic nutrition at the Institute for Integrative Nutrition, becoming a certified health coach.

The process was transformative. I found my answers, no longer take any prescription medicines, and have a much deeper understanding of how food exacerbates or improves upon the physical ailments I'm inclined to have. I understand how to eat best for my body.

I get great personal and professional satisfaction from helping others achieve similar results. It's stunning to see how simple food changes, eating more and tastier food, will quickly vanquish cravings, diminish or eliminate allergies, normalize gastrointestinal functions, and ease headaches, among other benefits.

-1-
YOU NEED MORE FOOD

You need more food.

You may be staring incredulously at the page, thinking that I'm nuts to say such a thing. Especially if you have some extra weight you'd like to lose, or are constantly trying to combat food cravings. Too much food seems like the problem, doesn't it?

It's not, and I'll say it again: You need <u>more</u> food. Real food provides really wonderful things: a variety of tastes and textures that result in satisfaction, consistent energy that allows your muscles and brain to work, and thousands of nutrients that grow, detoxify and repair your body and cells and allow them to function optimally.

The problem is that what you've been eating <u>isn't real food</u>. It probably has calories and may even taste good (then again it might not on either criteria!), but real, genuine food is increasingly rare in our food marketplaces. And when you don't eat <u>real</u> food, things get weird.

Americans are eating more processed foods than ever before, and it happened without most of us realizing it. When processed convenience foods hit the market in the 1950s most home cooks rejoiced at the newly available convenience. These exciting new products like canned soups and sauces saved time and effort and were an enormous hit. Since that time, highly processed food options have slowly replaced their unprocessed counterparts: breakfast cereals replaced breakfast porridge, fruit cups and fruit snacks replaced fresh fruit, and fast and frozen foods replaced home-cooked meals, just to name a few examples. Snacks and sugary drinks have exploded in size and variety; at the same time they increased as a percentage of daily calories.

My generation, Gen X, along with Gen Y, has grown up with processed foods being the normal and expected food options. Most baby boomers can still remember growing up eating seasonal foods, picking fruit and vegetables from their gardens or local farms, and their parents and grandparents spending significant amounts of time preparing meals from scratch. Younger generations are more likely to have grown up with boxed macaroni and cheese, canned pasta meals, an ever-expanding selection of boxed snack crackers and bars, and the latest bottled, boxed or canned beverage in the fridge.

Our daily staples, even those that most people wouldn't consider highly processed, are in fact in that category. Boxed breakfast cereals, most breads, bagels, pastas, pizza, chips and pretzels, pastries, lunch meats, fast and frozen foods, boxed or bagged snacks, and even restaurant foods have been processed to the point at which they no longer resemble nutritious food.

The U.S. Department of Agriculture's research shows that, on average, Americans are getting over sixty percent of their calories from processed and packaged foods such as chips and soda. Less than five percent are coming from plant foods like fruits, vegetables and seeds.

What is the result of this major shift of food sources? It has caught up to us in a major way; our youngest generation is the first ever in history not expected to outlive their parents, in fact they have a <u>lower life expectancy.</u>

Countries like the U.S. that consume these high levels of processed foods have exploding, all-time high rates of cancer, heart disease, obesity, diabetes, auto-immune diseases, Alzheimer's, and strokes, among other health problems. We are also taking more medications than ever to control symptoms like: high blood pressure, cholesterol, heartburn, headaches, chronic aches and pains, depression/anxiety, diarrhea, gas and constipation, and allergies.

It is not a coincidence. Our highly processed diets are making us more prone to these diseases and conditions. The problem with highly processed foods is that they are:

1. Deficient in nutrients, starving our bodies of thousands of health-promoting substances we need.
2. Manufactured into forms that our bodies digest differently, affecting our blood sugar and digestion in detrimental ways.
3. Full of additives that actively reduce health, including carcinogens, endocrine-disruptors, and other toxins.

When the majority of our diet comes from nutrient-void substances that have dangerous side effects to our body's natural processes, is it any wonder that so many people are feeling unwell?

The antidote to our highly-processed diet is eating one rich in nutrient-dense, delicious, unadulterated foods. Foods that flush your body with health-promoting nutrients, eliminate the physical stresses of the highly processed junk, and enable your body to do what it so desperately wants and knows how to do!

Food Doesn't Have to Be Complicated or Overthought

Sometimes the more you read about food, the more complicated and overwhelming it seems. In my training to become a health coach I learned about more than two hundred dietary theories. It can be exhausting to make sense of different diets, many of which directly contradict each other. Two of the most popular right now are the vegan and Paleo diets; you'd be hard-pressed to find two more dissimilar food philosophies! The Paleo, or "caveman's diet," is high in meat and includes no grains, dairy, or legumes such as beans and lentils. A vegan diet requires no meat or dairy and is therefore very high in grains and legumes as well as fruits and vegetables. Despite these differences both work extremely well for some people!

These vastly different ways of eating have existed for thousands of years and are reflected in historical diets. Before modern food production and world-wide shipping, people ate what they had access to. For example the traditional Inuit diet is comprised almost entirely of animal fats such as seal and whale blubber, with very little access to fresh plants. Okinowans in Japan, who have long been known to have one of the longest life expectancies in the world, eat very small amounts of animal foods and high amounts of rice and vegetables. Both traditional cultures experienced long and healthful lives with nearly non-existent rates of our common health problems, including heart disease and cancer.

The reality is that our bodies have evolved to function well on a variety of different kinds of diets and food sources. What the Inuits and the Okinawans' diets have in common is whole, unprocessed foods. This is certainly less sexy and mind-altering than many of the snazzy trademarked diets one can read about today, but it doesn't make it any less true!

I frequently receive questions such as, "What are the most important super-foods?" or "What five foods should I eat every day?" My answer is always the same: "I can't answer that!". There aren't five specific foods that everyone should eat every day, and there are hundreds of amazing nutrient-dense foods.

What I hope to accomplish with this book and through working with my clients is to change the lens through which you see and understand "food." Evaluating food on its "wholeness" will be more helpful than any other factor. For example, instead of stressing about finding low-calorie foods, you can focus on eating foods that have either no food label or only one (real food) ingredient (i.e. "broccoli") on the label.

When you begin eating primarily unprocessed foods, with even a basic level of food variety, things have a way of working themselves out. Did you know, for example, that you can survive almost entirely on potatoes, provided you eat the entire thing (most of the nutrients are in the skin) and have a little butter along with it? Whole potatoes have a surprising amount and variety of nutrients given their bad rap, and butter provides the missing vitamins A and D, along with the fats to assist in nutrient absorption and necessary omega-3s for the brain. This would not be possible with French fries or potato chips, for which the nutrient levels and the form of the food have been severely affected.

Relax and Return to an Intuitive Approach

One of the most amazing things that happens when you transition to a diet of primarily unprocessed foods is that your body's signals become much more logical and clear. This is especially true if you experience food cravings. I regularly meet with clients who are stressed and depressed, drained from their battles with food. They believe their struggle to lose weight and/or feel better is the result of a lack of self-control. Food cravings, especially for carb-heavy, salty, or sugary snacks are frequently a factor. What they perceive as a personal will-power issue is what I recognize as a natural signal from the body that it is out of balance. Their bodies are asking for something that they are not getting, but the wires are a bit crossed.

The answer is not to forcefully restrict eating, but rather to change what is being eaten. When you eat whole foods you will be amazed at how effortlessly junk food cravings disappear, energy increases, and the discomforts you've been living with begin to fade. When my clients begin to talk about cravings for spinach, berries, or even red meat, I know that their bodies are coming into balance. These are cravings that have real meaning and value, but you're unlikely to get them if your body is too stressed and mixed up from too many processed foods.

Cravings aren't the only symptoms that can be eliminated with a whole foods diet. Issues like migraines, inflammation-related conditions, stomach and gastro-intestinal symptoms, mood issues like depression and anxiety, and even fertility are also diet-related. Shifting to an unprocessed diet can alleviate many of these conditions within weeks. When I recently offered a 12-day cleanse program that only allowed unprocessed foods on the menu, the most commonly reported results were improved digestion, reduced food cravings, clearer sinuses, improved mental clarity and better sleep. One hundred percent of participants reported feeling better eating unprocessed foods.

Due to our nationwide obesity epidemic, most medical professionals are urging us to focus on portion-control, to "eat less." I disagree with this recommendation. I say eat more, and I mean that literally. When you transition to whole, unprocessed foods your portion sizes will <u>need</u> to increase, because the calorie density of unprocessed foods is less than processed foods. You will be able to fill your plates with the foods recommended in this book and eat until you're satisfied. Your body will come into balance and once again be able to tell you naturally when it is full and what foods it needs next. Your mind will be alleviated of that burden, which is an incredibly wonderful relief.

Real Food is Really Amazing

It is time to start loving our food, really loving it. Real food is amazing!

For too long we've been encouraged to think of foods in terms of their calories and grams of fat, carbohydrates, and protein. <u>These days have got to end.</u> This limited view of food does not nearly give it the credit it deserves. Food does not just have four limited properties. It has tens of thousands—if not more.

Well-known Functional Medicine expert Dr. Mark Hyman recently posted on his Facebook page a true or false question: T/F - 750 calories of soda has the same effect on the body as 750 calories of broccoli. Of course, it's false! A whole book could probably be written on just how different the effects would be of these two foods alone, but in general the soda is going to have a negative effect: causing inflammation, blood sugar spikes and a roller coaster of cravings. The broccoli can have substantial beneficial effects: helping the body to detoxify, providing a wealth of nutrients, and even preventing cancer formation. <u>Besides being inadequate, thinking of food in terms of calories and fat grams sucks all of the soul out of food and makes it no fun.</u>

One of the biggest differences between natural whole foods and highly processed foods is the amount of nutrients they provide. "Nutrients" may sound boring, but what I'm talking about here is <u>power</u>. Food, through its nutrients, has incredible power! Power to heal, power to protect, and power to refresh, renew and restore health and vibrancy. By eating nutrient-dense foods you can literally fortify yourself against aging and disease as well as exert a significant amount of control over how you feel on a daily basis.

This is how I like to think about food, for its breadth of beneficial properties, as well as for its flavor and the enjoyment of eating.

When people talk about "food as medicine," it's the medicinal role of various nutrients they're referring to. To really appreciate the powerful benefits of whole foods, it's helpful to know a little bit about the many nutrients they provide.

Vitamins, Minerals and Phytonutrients are Nature's Medicine

For quite some time, we've known about certain vitamins and minerals and that having low levels of these nutrients can cause health problems. Most of us grew up with some basic understanding of a few of those vitamins and minerals. Calcium is a good example; many women make conscious food choices, or take supplements, to ensure that they get enough calcium for strong bones. You may also be aware that vitamin C is good for the immune system, and drink orange juice or take vitamin c supplements when you have a cold.

This is all well and good, but foods from nature contain <u>thousands</u> of nutrients, including vitamins, minerals, and phytonutrients that contribute to our well-being. Our reliance on supplements and "fortified foods" (which are simply foods with vitamin and mineral supplements added to them) just can't cut it, for two reasons. First, we can't possibly supplement all of the thousands of nutrients that occur in natural foods. There are simply too many (not to mention, it's quite possible that many important nutrients are yet undiscovered!). Secondly, supplemental nutrients don't act the same way as those found in natural foods. Many nutrients act synergistically with others: food delivers a complex package that is digested and utilized in the body in ways that we can't replicate in the lab.

Like anybody, I would love to eat pizza and ice cream all day and simply rely on my multivitamin for vibrant health. (Pizza is my favorite food, and ice cream is a close second.) Unfortunately, it just doesn't work that way. In some cases, supplemental nutrients have even been shown to be harmful, either because the dosage can become too high, or because a synthetic form of the nutrient used in vitamins has harmful side effects. These downsides are very rare in natural foods.

Your diet and "nutritional status," in other words, how many nutrients you have in that body of yours, affects literally every physical process your body has. It affects your mood, your energy level, how effective your immune system is, how fast your muscles repair, how strong your heart is, your digestion, etc. With our current diets, a majority of Americans are deficient in several vitamins and minerals, and are certainly getting insufficient levels of phytonutrients.

Somehow the protective and healing role of foods and their nutrients has become undervalued. Perhaps it is because we've become a society that relies on medicine to cure disease, and perhaps we simply know much more today than we did in past decades about the number of nutrients and the breadth of ways they positively impact the body. Either way, it is time to start appreciating these miracles of nature.

Are You Getting Enough?

The most significant factor resulting in our extreme nutrient deficiency is our reliance on processed foods. Many, if not most nutrients, including vitamins, minerals and phytonutrients, are either removed or damaged via modern processing techniques, or simply don't exist in commonly processed foods. Eating a highly processed diet starves your body of micronutrients that it needs, making you more prone to disease, aging, and physical and emotional ailments.

Vitamins and Minerals

The following chart shows various essential vitamins and minerals, what they do in the body, signs of deficiency, and whether Americans are likely to be deficient.

Vitamin and Mineral Deficiency Information

Vitamin	Found in Foods	Deficiencies Can Cause	What It Does	% Americans Deficient*
Vitamin A	Sweet potatoes, carrots, dark leafy greens, melons, peppers, fish, liver, eggs	Weakened immune function, blindness and eye problems, skin problems, diabetes, low birth weight babies *A recent study indicated that many children may be getting too much synthetic vitamin A through fortified breakfast cereals	Supports vision, the immune system and inflammatory responses, required for normal cell growth, important for reproductive processes	Low overall, with higher risk of deficiency in carotenoid forms of vitamin A in diets that lack fresh fruits and vegetables
Vitamin C	Papaya, peppers, broccoli, Brussels sprouts, strawberries, pineapple, many other fresh fruits and vegetables	Impaired immune function, asthma, gout, allergies	A powerful antioxidant that protects against free radical damage, improves iron absorption, produces collagen, helps to make some neurotransmitters such as serotonin	**High,** if not eating several servings of fresh fruits and vegetables each day
Vitamin D	Fatty fish such as salmon and sardines, cod liver oil, egg yolks, liver, and generated by the body with exposure to natural light	Weakened immune system, higher risk of cancer, rickets in children and softened bones, reduced calcium and mineral absorption (can lead to osteoporosis), depression, asthma, rheumatoid arthritis	Bone health, blood sugar control, health of the immune system including infection and cancer prevention	**High,** with estimates for how many Americans are deficient in vitamin D are as high as 80 to 90%
Vitamin E	Sunflower seeds, almonds, spinach, various greens, avocado, fatty fish, liver, eggs	Low levels associated with higher risk of cancer, heart disease, Alzheimer's Disease, eye health, menstrual pain, diabetes, pre-eclampsia, and rheumatoid arthritis	Powerful antioxidant that can potentially reduce the risk of cancer and heart disease as well as reduce aging. Also helps the body use vitamin K and make red blood cells.	**High,** with as many as 92% of men and 98% of women estimated to get only 50% the DRI

Vitamin K	Kale, spinach, other green vegetables, liver, also produced by intestinal bacteria	Abnormal blood clotting, higher risk of bone fracture	Can improve insulin resistance and protect blood vessels	**High** risk of mild deficiency
Thiamin (B1)	Sunflower seeds, various beans, peas and legumes, oats	Easily harmed by food processing, deficiencies are common. Causes Beriberi; weakness and mental symptoms, and linked to Alzheimer's and Parkinson's disease	Central to energy metabolism and supporting the brain/nervous system	20% of Americans estimated as deficient
Riboflavin (B2)	Soybeans, beet greens, spinach, yogurt, mushrooms, eggs, asparagus, turkey, almonds	Iron deficiency anemia, migraines, congestive heart failure, high homocysteine, cataract, Parkinson's disease, hypertension	Critical for energy production, antioxidant activity, metabolizing iron	Lower, estimated at 2%
Niacin (B3)	Tuna, chicken, turkey, salmon, lamb, beef, sardines, peanuts, shrimp, brown rice, crimini mushrooms, asparagus	Pellagra, high cholesterol, osteoarthritis, Schizophrenia, Type I diabetes	Important for energy production and as an antioxidant that protects against tissue damage	Low, since niacin has been added to processed grains, dietary deficiency is low
Vitamin (B6)	Tuna, turkey, beef, chicken, salmon, bell peppers, cabbage, sweet potatoes, spinach, bananas	Anemia, morning sickness and PMS, epilepsy, depression, ADHD, asthma, fibrocystic breasts	Carbohydrate metabolism, brain health including producing neurotransmitters serotonin, GABA and dopamine, liver detoxification	Estimated at about 25% of Americans, with women and African Americans at higher risk
Folate (folic acid)	Lentils, romaine lettuce, various beans, spinach, asparagus, turnip greens and broccoli	Fatigue, forgetfulness, depression, and other mental/cognitive symptoms, anemia, insomnia, risk of cardiovascular disease and Alzheimer's, osteoporosis	Supports red blood cell formation, proper nerve function, prevents osteoporosis, prevents dementia, critical to healthy pregnancy/neural tube formation, preventative of breast cancer	Low, since folic acid has been fortified into processed grains in 1998, however naturally occurring folate may have more health benefits than the synthetic folic acid

Vitamin	Found in Foods	Deficiencies Can Cause	What It Does	% Americans Deficient*
Vitamin B12	Sardines, salmon, tuna, cod, lamb, scallops, shrimp, beef, yogurt	Fatigue, depression, memory loss, migraine, asthma, incontinence, loss of taste and smell	Critical to DNA production, brain and nervous system health, including production of serotonin and other neurotransmitters	Low overall, but high for vegans and those with malabsorption
Biotin (B7)	Peanuts, almonds, sweet potato, eggs, onions, oats, tomatoes, carrots, walnuts	Blood sugar regulation problems, skin rash	Hair and nail health, blood sugar regulation	Low
Pantothenic acid (B5)	Mushrooms, avocado, sweet potato, lentils, dried peas, poultry, broccoli, yogurt, many other foods	High cholesterol, chronic fatigue	Important for producing energy and metabolizing fats	Very low risk
Choline	Shrimp, eggs, scallops, poultry, fish, beef, collard greens	Liver damage, possible pregnancy complications	Critical for cell membrane growth, cell signaling, transmitting nerve impulses, methylation	Risk of deficiency is believed to be low, but higher in strict vegetarians
Calcium	Dairy products, tofu, sesame seeds, sardines, collard greens, spinach, various other leafy greens	Osteoporosis, high blood pressure	Critical for strong bones, acid-alkaline balance regulation	**High,** with the biggest risk in adolescent girls and elderly women. Calcium status can be worsened by low levels of Vit D, which enables absorption
Iron	Red meat, soybeans, lentils, spinach, sesame seeds, garbanzo and lima beans, olives, swiss chard	Anemia, fatigue, ADD/ADHD	Transports oxygen to tissues and supports energy production	More common in women than men, at about 10% Risk in kids around 15%

Mineral	Food Sources	Deficiency Symptoms	Function	Deficiency Prevalence
Iodine	Sea vegetables, scallops, cod, yogurt, shrimp, sardines, salmon, eggs	Infertility, thyroid disease, goiter	Plays a critical role in creating hormones in the thyroid gland	**High,** and increasing substantially in recent years
Magnesium	Spinach, swiss chard, other leafy greens, various seeds and beans, summer squash, quinoa	Migraines, depression, osteoporosis, constipation, fatigue, diabetes, heart disease, anxiety, asthma, muscle cramps	Critical for metabolism and energy production, creating and maintaining bones, controls inflammation, regulates blood sugar levels, maintaining nervous system function	**Very high;** average diets do not contain the recommended daily value
Zinc	Oysters, beef, spinach, asparagus, mushrooms, lamb, sesame seeds, pumpkin seeds, garbanzo beans	Impaired immune system, male infertility, depression	Important for immune system, skin health, sensory organs such as taste and vision, and male reproductive health	Low, but higher in vegetarian or vegan diets high in processed foods
Selenium	Seafood, poultry, beef, brazil nuts	Thyroid disease and a potential link to increased risk for cancer *Too much selenium can be dangerous	An important antioxidant that helps to regulate the body's detoxification systems and reduce oxidative stress, and critical to thyroid health	Low
Copper	Sesame and sunflower seeds, cashews, mushrooms, garbanzo beans, lentils, walnuts	Anemia, high cholesterol, fatigue, lowered immune system, osteoporosis, arthritis	Helps to build strong bones and tissues, maintain blood volume, balance cholesterol levels, and prevent anemia, and produce energy. Is the cofactor of an important antioxidant ("SOD") in the body.	**Moderate to High,** estimated at 25-50% of Americans
Manganese	Cloves, oats, brown rice, garbanzo beans, spinach, pineapple, pumpkin seeds, rye	Itchy skin rash, blood sugar control problems, abnormal bone development	Important for bone production, skin formation and protection, blood sugar control, and antioxidant activity	Believed to be low

Vitamin	Found in Foods	Deficiencies Can Cause	What It Does	% Americans Deficient*
Chromium	Broccoli, beets, barley, oats, green beans, garlic, mushrooms, romaine lettuce, onions	Insulin resistance/blood sugar regulation problems	Key role in regulating blood sugar	Research isn't clear on ideal levels of chromium or likelihood of deficiency
Potassium	Beet greens, swiss chard, lima beans, sweet potatoes, potatoes, soy beans, spinach, lentils	High blood pressure, stroke, kidney stones, fatigue	Helps to maintain normal blood pressure and kidney health	**High**, estimated at 98% of Americans with highest risk for women and African Americans
Misc				
Omega 3 Fatty Acids (DHA, EPA, and ALA)	Flax seeds, walnuts, sardines, salmon, soybeans, shrimp	Increased risk of cardiovascular disease, inflammation-related disorders and diseases, ADD/ADHD, depression, diabetes, migraines, cognitive problems	Powerful regulator of inflammation (anti-inflammatory), important for brain function (DHA is 9–12% of our brain matter)	**High** The ratio of Omega-6 to Omega-3 fatty averages is the significant factor. The average ratio is estimated at somewhere between 20:1 and 8:1, with an ideal range of 4:1 to 2:1

Source: www.whfoods.org

*deficiency is determined by not meeting Dietary Reference Intake (DRI)

Powerhouse Phytonutrients Prevent Cancer, Boost Immunity, and More

If you've heard about antioxidants, lycopene in tomatoes, or resvertrol in red wine, you've heard about phytonutrients. While phytonutrients themselves aren't new, our knowledge about them is relatively recent. In a way, they're the sexy new nutrients researchers are excited to learn all about. They are immensely fascinating.

Phytonutrients are plant-based chemicals, many of which affect our cells in ways that are biologically beneficial. There are literally tens of thousands of phytonutrients, too many to name individually. Each plant produces hundreds of different phytonutrients and their effects on our bodies are wide-ranging.

One of the most well understood roles that many phytonutrients play is their ability to act as antioxidants. Antioxidants are incredible in their ability to protect our cells from damage and aging. They do this by neutralizing free radicals, which are volatile compounds that damage cells and sometimes our DNA.

Imagine an old-school Pac-Man arcade game, where Pac-Man is an antioxidant, and all of the things Pac-Man eats are free-radicals in the body. Antioxidant Pac-Man's job is to roam around your body and eat up the free-radicals, saving your body from harm, and the more Pac-Mans you have, the more free radicals get eaten. Free radicals come from the environment, pollution, stress, and even rigorous exercise. While some free radical sources, such as cigarette smoke, are avoidable, many may not be. Eating foods with plenty of antioxidants is a way to fortify your body and enable it to ward off those stresses on a cellular level. Because free radical damage to DNA can be the genesis of cancer, antioxidants can be an incredibly powerful tool.

Other phytonutrients enable cell-to-cell communication, and some alter the expression of our genes in beneficial ways.

In her incredibly informative book, <u>Eating on the Wild Side</u>, Jo Robinson details hundreds of studies that demonstrate the potency of phytonutrients to provide various health benefits. This list of benefits comes directly from those studies:

<u>Benefits of Phytonutrients</u>

- Support the immune system
- Support eye health, prevent macular degeneration and cataracts
- Lower the risk of cancer
- Improve liver function
- Reduce inflammation in the body
- Reduce the risk of asthma

- Reduce the risk of coronary heart disease
- Extend life span
- Thin the blood
- Improve mood
- Boost immunity
- Fight viruses and bacteria
- Protect against an aging brain
- Improve weight loss
- Lower LDL cholesterol
- Improve athletic performance
- Inhibit tumor growth
- Lower blood sugar levels
- Reduce blood pressure

The following is a chart showing a few of the most well-studied phytonutrients, what foods they're found in, and some of their effects on the body. One helpful rule of thumb regarding phytonutrients is that they tend to be concentrated in richly colored foods. Richly colored berries, bright root vegetables such as sweet potatoes and carrots, and dark leafy greens such as red lettuces and green kale are wonderful sources of antioxidants. Even grains, such as red and purple rices, can be loaded with antioxidants.

Phytonutrient Health Benefits

Phytonutrient type	Examples	Found In	Health Benefits
Carotenoids (more than 600)	Alpha and beta-carotenes, lycopene	Yellow, orange and red colored fruits and dark leafy greens	Act as antioxidants, neutralizing free radicals that cause tissue damage, protect against cancer, prevent eye problems
Polyphenols	Flavonoids inlcluding quercetin, catechins, cyanidin,	Onions, tea, wine, apples, cranberries, grapes, lentils, red apples and pears, blackberries, blueberries, purple rice and corn	Reduces the risk of asthma, cancer, coronary heart disease, lowers cholesterol, blocks inflammation
	Isoflavonoids including genistein	Purple potatoes	Lowers risk of breast and prostate cancer and reduces blood pressure
	Stilbenoids including resvertrol	Grape skins, wine	Reduces the risk of heart disease and cancer, extends life span
	Phenolic acids including ellagic acid	Strawberries, raspberries, pomegranates	Protects against cancer
Glucosinolates	Precursors to isothiocyanates, organosulfides, indoles, Allicin	Cruciferous vegetables such as collard greens and kale, broccoli, and many others	Prevents the growth of cancer
Betalains	Betacyanins, Betaxanthings	Beets, swiss chard	Blocks cancer proliferation in the pancreas, stomach, lungs, and brain

Source: Eating on the Wild Side, Jo Robinson

Conclusion

Every meal is an opportunity to put something delicious and healing into your body. If you look at the foods in which these vitamins, minerals and phytonutrients are abundant, they're not pretzels, crackers, or my beloved pizza. They're not breakfast cereals, breakfast bars, or snack packs. They're whole fruits, vegetables, legumes, meats, fish, eggs, etc. This is what I mean by real food.

While there are hundreds or thousands of studies on the health benefits of various foods, you truly don't need to be an expert or well-read on the subject to benefit from the foods. Nor do you need to spend big bucks on exotic superfoods or supplements. Most natural, unprocessed foods offer benefits in the form of vitamins, minerals and phytonutrients, and making those foods the mainstay of your diet will have a bigger impact on your health than any other change you can make.

In the coming chapters, you'll learn why heavily processed foods do not provide the same benefits and how to select and prepare unprocessed foods in an easy and affordable way.

-2-
THE PROBLEMS WITH PROCESSED FOOD

Demystifying Processed Food: What is Processed?

Food has been "processed" in some manner since we've been on earth. Sun-drying tomatoes or peppers, salting meats, and fermenting cabbage into sauerkraut are all forms of processing, or in these cases specifically, preserving foods. To make it through winters, droughts, or travel, we humans have had to preserve foods that became available in harvest times so that they'd last us through several months.

In other instances foods were processed to become more digestible. Masa harina is a form of cornmeal that is used to make tortillas, tamales, and other staple foods in South and Central America. It is made from maize, a difficult to digest form of corn, that is soaked in lime water. The lime water loosens the tough maize hulls from the edible portion of the grain and makes the kernel more nutritious by making the niacin and calcium, among other nutrients, more bio-available. Other types of "processing" that improve digestibility are soaking and sprouting grains and seeds, and fermenting.

Preservation methods that are still popular today include canning, drying, and freezing. Canned jams and tomato sauces, frozen vegetables, and dried fruits or jerkies are still widely available and quite useful.

I remember my Mom canning pears, peaches and applesauce that we'd enjoy during the winter as a treat. But I personally never had to can, ferment, or dry any food to ensure that I wouldn't starve or get scurvy in the winter. In some ways this is too bad, because processing traditional foods in certain ways has played an important role in our ability as a species to survive, and continues to be important both nutritionally and culturally. Some of the traditional preservation techniques, such as fermenting, soaking or sprouting, that improve the nutritional content of various foods could stand to make a come-back!

Today's Food Processing Uses Other Approaches

In general, the above are not the forms of heavily processed foods that I refer to in this book. Modern processing techniques, which are overwhelmingly destructive, actually denature foods, strip them apart literally, remove their nutrients, change their physical structure, and frequently add chemicals or other substances that cause harm to the body. This type of widespread food processing is relatively new.

The technology to process whole grains into white flour wasn't created until the late 19th Century, but even then took several decades to become mainstream. Industrially processed, pre-made food products really hit the markets in the 1950s and 1960s, and have slowly but surely taken over market share from more traditional unprocessed foods. In general, there has been a transition of receiving one's food from a small to medium sized local farm, of which there used to be tens of thousands, to most food coming from just a few enormous industrially-sized farms and processors. Heavy food processing has enabled this change, and it's also required by it.

Most people don't realize just how processed their diets are. The cultural changes that have dictated which foods are "normal" have happened over the course of a few generations, and have now reached the point where processed foods are the default - the norm. With the average American eating more industrially processed food than anything else, at an estimated 60 percent of their overall diet, processed food is simply our food. We've seen an unprecedented rise in diseases such as diabetes and cancer that have risen right along with this trend.

So what foods are heavily processed?

Not surprisingly, most fast foods, pre-made frozen dinners, chips, snack bars and crackers, sodas and industrially made baked goods are highly processed.

But so are any products made from refined flours, such as breads, bagels, crackers, pastas, pizzas, breakfast cereals, pretzels, and baked goods. Even if they're coming from your own kitchen or a local bakery; if they're made from refined flours, they're highly processed from the start.

Dairy, a seemingly straight-forward food, is so highly processed it's barely recognizable from its original milk. Yogurts, many cheeses and cheese products, and even low-fat milk are some of the worst offenders.

Highly processed meats include most sausages, bacon, lunch meats, pepperoni and salamis, and even ground meats.

Virtually any snack food that comes in a bag or box, most all meal-replacement bars or powders, and any bottled beverage - including water in some cases - are highly processed.

What about the billion-dollar-plus market for so-called "health foods"? These are some of the absolutely most highly processed foods and ingredients available, including gluten-free baked goods, protein bars and powders, smoothies, and meal replacements of various shapes and flavors.

I list all of these not to depress you or make you feel like there are no foods left to eat. That couldn't be further from the truth. Actually, when you transition to a diet of unprocessed foods what you'll find is that <u>the variety of foods that you eat increases enormously</u>. Processed food products tend to pull from the same short list of ingredients: namely white flour, sugar, salt, some dairy, and various additives. They are processed into hundreds or thousands of different forms, giving the illusion of variety, but what ultimately enters your body is limited. Except for the thousands of chemicals approved for use in foods, that list is actually very extensive. What irony that with real foods we'd be eating thousands of phytonutrients or phytochemicals, but with processed foods we're eating thousands of unnatural chemicals!

Eating the above highly processed foods causes physical problems, for three main reasons:

1. Processing foods reduces nutrients.
2. Processing foods changes the way your body digests the food.
3. Processing adds substances that are detrimental to the body.

Food Processing Reduces Nutrients

One confusing and seemingly contradictory phenomena is that people who are overweight or obese are frequently malnourished; this is a side effect of a diet that is high in processed foods. However, you don't need to be overweight to be suffering from nutrient deficiencies as a result of a processed diet. Personally I know that a magnesium deficiency was contributing to my migraines. I routinely see clients improve various symptoms with a high-nutrient diet that comes from whole foods.

Eating a standard American diet of highly processed foods will almost always result in nutrient deficiencies in vitamins, minerals, and certainly phytonutrients. This is due to two main reasons:

1. Food processing techniques reduce the number of nutrients.
2. The most common highly processed foods tend to be low in nutrients to begin with.

——————— Caroline's Story ———————

Caroline, a successful small business owner in her late twenties, was experiencing multiple weekly migraines and daily digestive problems when she sought my help. An avid athlete and generally busy person, Caroline was tired of these issues reducing her quality of life, and she had exhausted traditional treatment optional including several different types of migraine medications, Botox injections, and even nutritional supplements. These interventions had small to moderate success, however Caroline didn't want to be on so many medications and the results were inconsistent.

Caroline had been experiencing her debilitating migraines since childhood, as many as two or three each week, and she was also troubled daily with bloating, constipation, and other forms of indigestion. She also experienced strong food cravings, especially after dinner, and was worried about her weight fluctuating. Though she kept daily food and headache journals, she hadn't been able to make any clear connections between specific foods and her symptoms. Like many clients, she suspected that she would simply have to live with these symptoms forever.

With her busy schedule Caroline had developed a routine of convenience. Though she enjoyed homemade food, it wasn't the mainstay of her diet. She skipped breakfast, ate hot dogs, convenience soups, or restaurant meals for lunch, and either a homemade, meat-and-potatoes based dish or take-out for dinner.

Together, Caroline and I identified a series of changes that would fit into her busy routine. She significantly increased her vegetable intake, especially powerful leafy green vegetables, started eating breakfast and more substantial lunches from home-cooked ingredients, and added a significant amount of variety to her diet, including new grains and legumes. Another big change was to eliminate processed forms of meats, substituting in unprocessed varieties, as well as fresh fish once or twice a week. Finally, Caroline completed an elimination diet that identified a strong dairy intolerance.

With these changes, Caroline was able to completely eliminate her digestive symptoms, including her nearly lifelong constipation. Her migraines dropped from several times per week to 2 or 3 per month. With the new foods added to her routine, Caroline has, with rare exception, nearly eliminated processed foods.

Food Processing Reduces the Nutrients in Food

Our Daily Bread

The best example of how food processing reduces the amount of nutrition in food is our country's most popular staple, our daily bread: wheat. On average Americans eat over 130 pounds of wheat per person, per year. This is over a pound of wheat every three days. For many Americans on a higher carbohydrate diet it's much more.

A kernel of whole, unprocessed wheat looks a little like a grain of brown rice: It's small, oblong, and light brown. It has three distinct parts: the bran, the germ, and the starchy endosperm. In its unprocessed form, wheat is a good source of many nutrients, including manganese, fiber, copper, magnesium and pantothenic acid, as well as several phytonutrients. It's well known that eating whole grains is related to lower rates of various cancers, especially colon cancer, less heart disease, and a healthier weight.

However, most Americans get their wheat in flour form, and most flours aren't made from the entire kernel of whole wheat. Most wheat in the U.S. is processed into 60 percent extraction, bleached flour. This means that 40 percent of the wheat kernel is removed, and the remaining endosperm is bleached to achieve a whiter white color. Unfortunately for those of us who eat the 60 percent extracted flour, the 40 percent that has been removed includes the wheat bran and wheat germ, which contain nearly all of the nutrients. In the extraction process, nearly all of the fiber is removed, as is over half of vitamins B1, B2, B3, vitamin E, folic acid, calcium, phosphorus, zinc, copper, and iron. The phytonutrients, which reside in the darkly colored bran and germ, are also removed.

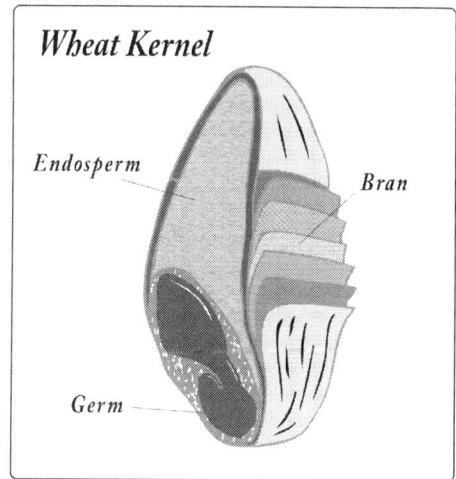

Wheat Kernel

Endosperm

Bran

Germ

This processed flour is confusingly called "enriched," because it is now legally required for manufacturers to add back in some of the vitamins that have been lost. However, only a small percentage of just a few of the vitamins that have been lost are replaced. The result is a nutritionally voided food product that is a major dietary staple.

Why would food manufacturers do this? I get this question all the time at seminars. It actually makes perfect sense for them. The bran and the germ contain trace amounts of oils, which will go rancid once exposed to oxygen (ground into flour). Whole grain flours have a shelf life of approximately 3 to 6 months. White "enriched" flours will last at least two years. Food manufacturers rejoiced when this manufacturing process was perfected, because they no longer had to worry about a short shelf life for flours or products made from them, or conditions, such as higher temperatures, which could contribute to spoilage. It's about the money, the profit, the shareholders. It's better logistics and less product loss. It doesn't hurt that white flour products are more addictive, either.

Try checking out your food labels to see what kind of wheat is in your pantry. "Wheat", "wheat flour", and "enriched flour" all refer to this highly processed flour with the bran and germ removed. Your ingredient list must say "whole wheat" to ensure that the entire grain is included in the flour. One tricky marketing maneuver to look out for: if your bread label (or any other wheat product) says "whole wheat" on the front, legally it only needs to have 50 percent whole grains. The other 50 percent can be processed white flour. You'll need to read the ingredients label to see what's really in there, or choose a product that has "100 percent whole grains" on the front label.

Fruits and Vegetables

Fruits and vegetables are processed in a variety of ways, including freezing, canning or jarring, drying or dehydrating, and of course turning them into various food products such as applesauce or jams. The amount of nutrient loss that occurs can differ between the various fruits and vegetables, nutrients, and processing techniques, and not all processed produce is bad. That said, there are some generalizations regarding nutrient loss that can help you understand which options are best and which should be avoided.

Whole Is Best

Like grains, fruits and vegetables are usually best when their entire edible portion is present. A lot of the nutrients are in the skins. Canned fruits such as peaches and pears have frequently had their skins removed, which eliminates the many antioxidants you'd get from the whole fruits. Same goes for canned or otherwise processed potatoes. If the skin has been removed, so has a significant amount of its nutrition. I recently read an article advocating that you eat banana skins for their high number of nutrients, although I can't say I've gone this far myself.

Exposure to Water and Heat Equal Nutrient Loss

When fruits and vegetables are processed, one of the most significant areas of nutrient loss is water-soluble vitamins such as Vitamin C and B-complex vitamins. These are particularly sensitive to heat or can leach into water. For that reason, canning, jarring, and blanching (a quick boiling technique frequently used for vegetables before they're frozen) can dramatically reduce the amounts of various vitamins in canned and frozen produce. For example, canned mixed vegetables lose up to 67 percent of their vitamin C. In general, the longer the exposure to heat and water the more nutrient loss occurs; boiling spinach for 10 minutes results in more nutrition in the boiling liquid than the actual spinach. Tomatoes lose up to 70 percent of their folate when canned into tomato juice. For this reason, I generally recommend avoiding canned fruits and vegetables as a source of regular nutrition.

Frozen vegetables generally have slightly less nutrient loss. Although they've likely been blanched, their overall exposure to heat and water is usually less extensive than canned. While I prefer fresh vegetables to frozen, I do rely on frozen vegetables when fresh vegetables aren't available or are limited. Frozen broccoli and spinach can be a lifesaver, especially in the winter or on a busy night, but in the summer and fall I enjoy fresher options.

Processed fruit and vegetable products are even worse when these two factors are combined. For example, applesauce and juice that have been made without skins and have been cooked for extensive times, as they usually are, are nearly nutritionally void. One study shows only 10% of the flavonols and 3 percent of the catechins from the original apples remained in the apple juice. Chlorogenic acid, one of the most heat-stable phytonutrients, was reduced by 50 percent. Most vitamin C remaining in commercially available apple sauce has actually been added back in in vitamin form. You'll see this as ascorbic acid on the food label. The same goes for highly processed fruit cups which are often made even worse by adding sugary syrup. Other examples of nutritionally void fruit or vegetable products include fruit snacks, anything where the main fruit ingredient is a reduced fruit juice (this is basically just sugar), or products that use so little fruit that it's more of a marketing ploy, such as blueberry muffin or waffle mixes, which many times won't contain any traces of real fruit whatsoever.

How Do I Know If It's Highly Processed?

1. Has the food been broken into pieces/parts, with some of them removed?
2. Does it look very different from its natural form, when it was harvested from a plant or animal?
3. Has it been exposed to high-heat cooking?

Food Processing Changes How You Digest and Metabolize Food

Most people have experienced a blood-sugar high, but could you be experiencing pro-longed daily blood sugar imbalances? Many processing techniques change foods' physical properties in ways that change how our bodies digest and metabolize the food. This is nearly always the difference between digesting an unprocessed food slowly versus digesting a processed food quickly. That might not sound like a big deal, but actually the blood sugar instability that this creates is at the root of our most common modern diseases, including cancer, cardio-vascular disease, chronic inflammation and related conditions, obesity and diabetes, and ovulation-related infertility. Low glycemic diets, in which foods are digested slowly, are associated with lower risk of all of the above.

Your body has two main things it wants to get from your food: the first is nutrients; and the second is calories for energy. Every cell in your body needs energy to function, and your body's energy currency is glucose, otherwise known as blood sugar. When you eat, your body turns the calories in food into glucose that then enters your blood stream. From there, your pancreas releases insulin which is the "key" that allows your cells to unlock their "doors" and let in glucose. At that point they happily go about their business.

Most unprocessed foods will be turned into energy (blood sugar) relatively slowly. Your body likes this; it provides a nice, constant source of energy for your brain and the rest of your body and your pancreas chugs along releasing insulin at a comfortable rate.

If you've ever experienced a sugar high, inevitably followed by a sugar low, you know what it feels like to have eaten foods that break down into blood sugar very quickly. Personally, I'll feel euphoric for twenty to thirty minutes, then pretty miserable for the next few hours, with low energy and sleepiness. Foods high in sugar and starches can have this effect. It's very uncomfortable.

Blood sugar highs often feel great; they cause a bound in energy and a surge in serotonin to your brain that makes us happy. However, the "low" usually causes extreme fatigue, sleepiness, an inability to concentrate, and a depressed or anxious mood. This is what happens when too much glucose floods into your blood stream; your pancreas is forced to crank out a large amount of insulin very quickly to clear the glucose from your blood stream (chronically high levels of blood glucose are dangerous and can cause inflammation and arterial damage), and frequently, the result is an over-compensation and low blood sugar.

All too often sugar highs that result in sugar lows lead people to <u>again</u> find quick sources of sugar, re-starting the cycle. In this way, blood sugar instability is a vicious cycle that can continue on throughout the day, causing mood swings and leading to chronic health problems.

You don't have to be drinking soda after soda to be on this roller coaster. Check out the glycemic index below, which is a measure of how fast your body turns different foods into blood sugar. Foods are ranked on a scale of 1 to 100, with 100 being the fastest possible transition to blood sugar (actually, the only food with a 100 is actual glucose, because it takes zero time to become glucose). A zero on the scale would be a food that never turns into glucose; essentially one that you can't digest, such as aspartame.

Sugar isn't the only high-glycemic food, in fact white flour will produce a sugar high <u>faster</u> than table sugar! <u>That means that a piece of white toast or a bagel (GI=73) will actually give you a worse sugar high than a can of soda</u> (GI=63). Even more shocking, so will some whole-grain breads (GI=71). Another important number in this chart is the glycemic load. This number takes into account the averages calories in a given food. For example, carrots have a high glycemic index, but they're unlikely to give you too much of a sugar high, because a serving of carrots is so low in calories. You'd have to eat a few pounds to equal the glycemic load of a higher-calorie food.

Food processing increases the glycemic index of foods relative to their natural state in a few different ways. Food processing:

1.   Increases the surface area of absorbable calories
2.   Removes fiber
3.   Removes or limits fat

Glycemic Index for Common Foods

Food	Glycemic Index	Serving Size in grams	Glycemic Load
Bagel, white, frozen	72	70	25
Baguette, white, plain	95	30	15
Coarse barley bread, 75-80% kernels, average	34	30	7
Pumpernickel bread	56	30	7
50% cracked wheat kernel bread	58	30	12
White wheat flour bread	71	30	10
Whole wheat bread, average	71	30	9
Corn tortilla	52	50	12
Wheat tortilla	30	50	8
Beverages			
Coca Cola®, average	63	250 mL	16
Apple juice, unsweetened, average	44	250 mL	30
Cranberry juice cocktail (Ocean Spray®)	68	250 mL	24
Gatorade	78	250 mL	12
Orange juice, unsweetened	50	250 mL	12
Tomato juice, canned	38	250 mL	4
Breakfast cereals			
All-Bran™, average	55	30	12
Cornflakes™, average	93	30	23
Grapenuts™, average	75	30	16
Oatmeal, average	55	250	13
Instant oatmeal, average	83	250	30
Puffed wheat, average	80	30	17
Grains			
Pearled barley, average	28	150	12
Sweet corn on the cob, average	60	150	20
Couscous, average	65	150	9
Quinoa	53	150	13
White rice, average	89	150	43
Brown rice, average	50	150	16

Food	Glycemic Index	Serving Size in grams	Glycemic Load
Grains, con't			
Whole wheat kernels, average	30	50	11
Bulgur, average	48	150	12
Cookies and Crackers			
Graham crackers	74	25	14
Vanilla wafers	77	25	14
Rice cakes, average	82	25	17
Dairy			
Ice cream, regular	57	50	6
Ice cream, premium	38	50	3
Milk, full fat	41	250mL	5
Milk, skim	32	250 mL	4
Reduced-fat yogurt with fruit, average	33	200	11
Fruit			
Apple, average	39	120	6
Banana, ripe	62	120	16
Dates, dried	42	60	18
Grapefruit	25	120	3
Grapes, average	59	120	11
Orange, average	40	120	4
Peach, average	42	120	5
Pear, average	38	120	4
Prunes, pitted	29	60	10
Raisins	64	60	28
Watermelon	72	120	4
Beans and Nuts			
Blackeye peas, average	33	150	10
Black beans	30	150	7
Chickpeas, average	10	150	3
Chickpeas, canned in brine	38	150	9
Navy beans, average	31	150	9

Food	Glycemic Index	Serving Size in grams	Glycemic Load
Beans and Nuts, con't			
Kidney beans, average	29	150	7
Lentils, average	29	150	5
Soy beans, average	15	150	1
Cashews, salted	27	50	3
Peanuts, average	7	50	0
Pasta			
Fettucini, average	32	180	15
Macaroni, average	47	180	23
Macaroni and Cheese (Kraft)	64	180	32
Spaghetti, white, boiled, average	46	180	22
Spaghetti, white, boiled 20 min, average	58	180	26
Snacks			
Corn chips, plain, salted, average	42	50	11
Fruit Roll-Ups®	99	30	24
M & M's®, peanut	33	30	6
Microwave popcorn, plain, average	55	20	6
Potato chips, average	51	50	12
Pretzels, oven-baked	83	30	16
Snickers Bar®	51	60	18
Vegetables			
Green peas, average	51	80	4
Carrots, average	35	80	2
Parsnips	52	80	4
Baked russet potato, average	111	150	33
Boiled white potato, average	82	150	21
Instant mashed potato, average	87	150	17
Sweet potato, average	70	150	22
Yam, average	54	150	20

Source: Excerpted from www.health.harvard.edu

Increases the Surface Area

Many processing techniques, including grinding into flour, "puffing" or "popping," and grain-extracting turn foods from naturally low-glycemic to high-glycemic forms. Let's return to our whole grain wheat example. Wheat berries (unrefined whole wheat kernels) can be eaten quite nicely if soaked overnight and then boiled until tender. Eaten this way they're chewy, have a nice nutty flavor, and are delicious and satisfying to eat. Their glycemic index is 30, making them a low-glycemic food that will provide nice constant energy for hours to come.

Grinding that wheat kernel into a whole wheat flour exponentially increases the surface area for digestive enzymes to work to digest the food into glucose. When you chew the whole wheat berries, your teeth work to roughly increase the surface area so that your digestive enzymes can get to work. But your body still has to work through a fair amount of fiber and loosen the densely packed carbohydrates to break them down finely. In the case of whole grain flour, the work has been done for you; you can practically let fluffy whole grain bread dissolve in your mouth. Fluffy whole grain wheat bread has a glycemic index of 71, an enormous increase from 30 for the wheat berries.

White bread, made from processed and enriched white flour has a glycemic index that is marginally higher, at 73. In both the whole wheat bread and white bread examples, the body has very little work to do to break down the food due to the extremely large surface area that flour provides. Flour products will all have a higher glycemic index than their original grains; this is true of any other flour as well, including oat flour, quinoa flour, barley flour, corn flour, etc.

One interesting exception to this rule is when flour products have essentially been compressed into a dense form of pasta or bread. Al dente fettucini, which is once again chewy and dense, has a glycemic index of 32. The glycemic index will increase if you cook it longer; spaghetti which has been boiled for 20 minutes, so is no longer al dente and has a thinner noodle, has a glycemic index of 58. Pita bread and tortillas also have a lower glycemic index than fluffier breads.

Some of the most highly processed and highly glycemic foods in our diets are breakfast cereals; a food group most people believe to be a healthy start to the day. Corn flakes have a whopping glycemic index of 93, Raisin Bran is 62, and even GrapeNuts is 75! If you've ever eaten a bowl of cereal and been hungry only an hour later, this is why. The grains used in breakfast cereals come from highly processed grains and then are frequently "extruded" from special machines into their cute little shapes, a process that further increases their surface area.

Grains are the most common food group to be processed in this way, but other foods occasionally are as well, such as potato and other vegetable chips and french fries.

Removes Fiber

Fiber has a unique ability to slow down digestion, and it's all-too-often removed from processed foods. As mentioned, the fiber is removed from grains in the refining process, but fiber is also removed when vegetables and fruits are peeled or juiced.

One surprising example of this is instant oatmeal and other instant cereals. Instant oatmeal has had much of its fiber removed, because fiber slows the absorption of water into the grain, slowing its cooking process. Instant oatmeal has a glycemic index of 83, versus regular rolled oats at 55. I've always found the idea of instant oatmeal to be a little silly. After all, you can cook rolled oats in the microwave in only 3 minutes.

Removes Fat

Fat, as well as fiber, is able to slow down digestion. This is why the highest foods on the glycemic index tend to be fat-free. The absolute highest glycemic foods are low-fiber, low-fat, highly processed carbs with a high surface area. Low-fat foods became the fad in the '90s, and they've been too slow to disappear. Low-fat cookies and crackers, cereals, breads, fruit snacks and rolls, and even dairy products can raise your blood sugar quickly.

It's useful to know that you can lower the glycemic index of some foods by adding fat. Pizza dough on its own has a glycemic index of 80, but add the cheese and toppings and it drops to the 50s. Regular ice cream has a glycemic index of 57, but premium brands that have added egg yolks and higher butterfat content are as low as 38. This is why it's suggested to put olive oil on your bread at restaurants if you indulge in the bread bowl. While it might seem counterintuitive to add the calories, it will satiate your hunger much more effectively to eat the fat, and will reduce a blood sugar rush and the accompanying low and rebound urges. Ultimately, you're much more likely to eat less overall.

The blood sugar roller-coaster is more serious than it might seem; more is at stake than occasional discomfort. Because so many of the processed foods we consume, even health-conscious individuals who tend to target lower fat options, are highly glycemic, many of us are experiencing a mild to moderate daily glycemic roller-coaster. A good way to know if this effects you is if you have a daily energy slump, which many people experience in the late afternoon. This is a tell-tale symptom of low-blood sugar.

The older I get, the more sensitive I am to blood sugar swings. For me they're a real factor affecting my energy level, my ability to concentrate, and my mood. The term "hangry", a combination of hungry and angry, is right-on. For others the effects are more serious, and over time blood sugar instability can lead to metabolic syndrome, a set of risk factors that raise the risks of Type II diabetes, cardiovascular disease, and stroke. But the problems and discomforts arising from blood sugar swings are much wider than those affected by these conditions. Mood problems such as depression and anxiety, ADD and ADHD, and hormonal conditions such as PCOS and infertility are also related to fluctuating blood sugar. Mood problems such as depression and anxiety, ADD and ADHD, and hormonal conditions such as PCOS (polycystic ovary syndrome) and infertility are also related to fluc¬tuating blood sugar.

How Do I Know If It's Highly Processed?
1. Is it made from finely ground flour?
2. Is it light and airy, and/or can it practically dissolve on your tongue?
3. Do you feel hungry shortly after eating it?

Becky's Story

Becky was a young professional in her early twenties with a bustling career and a loving husband. Despite her youth, Becky was experiencing fertility problems when she came to me for help with her food.

Becky ate a standard American diet, with lots of soda, fast food, and processed meals. She knew that her diet was poor, but despite some fatigue and difficulty sleeping the only physical symptoms she experienced were her irregular cycle and difficulty becoming pregnant.

A steak-and-potatoes girl, Becky hadn't had much exposure to a variety of fresh foods. She didn't particularly enjoy shopping or cooking, but she did enjoy eating and had a wonderful attitude about trying new things.

One of the first things we discussed was the importance of controlling her blood sugar in regulating the hormones responsible for fertility. Though Becky wasn't a sugar-craver and didn't usually eat snacks, she did drink up to eight sodas in a day, nearly always skipped breakfast, and the kinds of heavily processed meals she ate, including fast-food sandwiches and wraps, included hidden sugars and the kinds of carbohydrates that would certainly cause blood sugar swings.

Becky needed a dietary overhaul. We worked together for several months to implement new foods and routines for her busy schedule. She began to cook more at home with a wider variety of nutrient-dense foods, and started taking packed lunches to work. Her soda habit was replaced with beverages that provided nutrients as well as a more natural source of energy. She began starting her day with a nutritious breakfast, even if it was eaten in the car. She learned how to make better choices at restaurants.

I was delighted to see Becky and her husband really enjoy the new foods they were trying. All the while, her new diet normalized her blood sugar levels and flushed her body with valuable nutrients. She began to have better energy and lost some weight. Then, a couple months after we began working together she became pregnant. Today Becky has two healthy kids and credits her new diet with helping her become pregnant and sustain healthy pregnancies. She even mentioned with pleasure that she was able to introduce her kids to foods at six months of age that she didn't try until she was twenty-five.

Food Processing Adds Dangerous Substances

Increasingly our food is made up of ingredients that aren't actually food. There are more than ten thousand chemical food additives approved for use in the United States. These additives fall under several categories:

- Preservatives
- Antibacterials and fungicides
- Dough conditioners
- Dyes/food colorings
- Sweeteners, both sugar and artificial
- Flavor enhancers including salt and chemicals such as MSG
- Food "fillers" that add bulk

- Man-made fats such as trans fats or fat substitutes
- Stimulants such as caffeine

Why So Many Additives?

When real food ingredients are parsed up and processed to the point where they're a shadow of their former selves they lack flavor. Salt, sugar, and chemical flavor enhancers are needed to make these products taste like something. Sometimes people are surprised to taste something they enjoyed in childhood, only to realize that it takes like nothing but sugar or salt. In addition, manufacturers want to lengthen shelf life, save money by reducing more expensive ingredients, make their products more addictive, and alter the texture or other properties of their products.

While these additives serve logical purposes for food manufacturing companies, they range from reasonably safe to downright dangerous for consumers. You may assume, like I did, that all food additives require rigorous testing and approval, much like drugs do. (The FDA is the Food and Drug Administration, after all.) But many common additives, as well as some chemicals used for processing foods, have not been well-tested for human consumption, and some that have been "generally regarded as safe" (GRAS) have later been conclusively found to be quite dangerous, such as trans fats.

Shockingly, others that have been studied and found to have detrimental health effects are approved. Many food additives are known to cause cancer, act as hormones in the body, contribute to heart disease, strokes and diabetes, and act as neurotoxins. Some are just disruptive; one extremely common additive, xanthan gum, isn't dangerous, but causes diarrhea even in small quantities. That would be nice to know when you're buying your salad dressing or gluten-free bread, but food manufacturers aren't going to volunteer to put this on the label. They don't have to. Food manufacturers and the FDA justify the approval of these dangerous chemicals by arguing they're used in quantities too small to cause harm. But independent organizations that are not subject to industry pressure such as the Center for Science in the Public Interest, a science-based nutrition, food safety and health organization in Washington D.C., have issued strict warnings on many legalized chemicals.

Common Additives

Additive	Health Consequence	Found In
Salt	high blood sugar, cardiac events and stroke	Everything; processed meats, meals, soups, vegetables, etc
Sugar	metabolic syndrome, diabetes, inflammation, cancer, migraines, ADD/ADHD	Everything; processed sauces, meals, snacks, meats, breads, desserts, condiments, etc
Food coloring	Hyperactivity, asthma, cancer	A lot of childrens' foods, medicines, snacks, desserts, puddings and jellos
High-fructose corn syrup	metabolic syndrome, type II diabetes, cancer	Everything; processed condiments, sauces, drinks, snacks, breads, etc
Aspartame	metabolic syndrome, cancer	Low or no calorie drinks and foods, including breads, chewing gum, and others
MSG (monosodium glutamate)	headaches, migraines, digestive problems, flushing	Processed savory items including meats, spice mixes, chips or snacks, nuts, etc
Sodium benzoate	Hyperactivity, cancer	Soft drinks and sodas and other acidic foods
Sodium nitrites/ nitrates	gastric cancer	Preserved meats such as bacon, ham, sausasges
Trans fats	heart disease, type II diabetes, inflammation	Commercial baked goods, frostings, fried foods, fast-food ice cream drinks

By far the most common additives to processed foods are sugar and salt. These might sound harmless, but they're added in such large quantities, and to so many foods, that they're causing very real health problems. They're no-brainer additives to food companies; both sugar and salt are preservatives that make foods last longer on store shelves. They're both flavor enhancers, and sugar especially is addictive, causing consumers to come back for more.

Sugar

We eat insane amounts of sugar; <u>what our great-grandparents ate in one year, we now eat in less than one week.</u> The average American consumes over 150 pounds per year, three pounds per week, and over a half-cup per day, totally a third of their entire calorie intake. Two hundred years ago, the average American ate only two pounds in an entire year.

I believe sugar is wreaking more havoc on health in the U.S. than just about anything else. It's not just that sugar is "empty calories," it actually acts as a toxin in the body. Sugar contributes to well-known problems with weight and metabolic problems: metabolic syndrome, extra weight and obesity, and Type II diabetes. It also promotes general inflammation, mood problems like depression and anxiety, wicked food cravings, heart disease, hormonal problems such as acne and polycystic ovary syndrome (PCOS), and high-sugar diets are a known risk factor for cancer.

Sugar isn't just added to sweets where you'd expect it. It's added to condiments, sauces, yogurts, processed meats, baked beans, breads, and just about anything a factory touches. When people move to the U.S. from other countries, the overall sweetness of our foods often times makes them uncomfortable. I've seen clients who remove sugar from their diets eliminate migraines, lower decades-long high cholesterol, reduce chronic pain, lose weight, and generally feel significantly better.

Some nutritionists recommend lowering daily added sugars to about 100 calories per day for women and 150 calories per day for men, which is 25 grams and 38 grams, respectively. This is would be a major improvement for many, but it's still a lot of sugar.

I really relate to people who are sugar-addicted, because I was too, and I believe it played a heavy hand in my digestive and sinus issues. Sugar doesn't have to be completely stripped from your diet, and I'm not saying you can't enjoy a cookie or sweet treat occasionally. I do recommend you start paying attention to how much sugar you're consuming, especially from hidden sources in processed foods. It's quite likely the amount you're eating from hidden sources is affecting your health or causing cravings. Eliminating the hidden sources will make an enormously beneficial change to your wellness in ways that you might find surprising. And believe it or not your taste buds will change quickly. Many of my clients, after a few months on a low-sugar regime, will go back and try a food that they formerly loved, only to find it unpalatably sweet.

—————————— Sue's Story ——————————

Sue was a lovely lady in her mid-60s who was fed up with being addicted to sugar when I met her. She felt like a hostage to her sugar cravings. She resented how they caused her weight to fluctuate throughout the year. She was tired of the yo-yo dieting cycle, and described how her weight would increase during one part of the year (typically the holidays), then she would have to crack down and become very strict with herself to lose the weight throughout the summer. She was exhausted with the whole situation, and realized that her sugar addiction was causing physical and emotional stress. She described that sugar seemed to have a "heroin-like affect" on her. (This is something I hear frequently, although most clients are a bit incredulous to admit it, and feel it's "just them".)

Though Sue was very active, exercising typically five times per week, and was doing her best to eat a healthful diet, she estimated that she was eating up to 600 calories of sugar in a day. She also noted that she didn't sleep very well and had chronic acid reflux. Her active lifestyle also included regular traveling, entertaining kids and grandkids, and happy hour "dates" with her husband. She was very conscious about not wanting to change her lifestyle to accommodate any extreme dietary changes. This, I assured her, would not be necessary.

After carefully examining Sue's food diary over the course of a week or two, I realized that hidden sugars in processed foods, especially those consumed earlier in the day, were likely driving her sugar cravings. Seemingly healthy and even savory items, such as bran cereal and regular peanut butter are loaded with surprisingly high amounts of sugar. Our first step was to eliminate these, substituting them for items that didn't contain added sugars.

I also asked to her indulge another little trick of mine; integrating some bitter greens into her diet. In Traditional Chinese Medicine bitter and sweet flavors are opposites, and a lack of one can lead to cravings for the other (think of the ying-yang balance). Not only do bitter greens flush your body with nutrients, which can diminish cravings in general, but they also directly help to counter sugar cravings.

At her second appointment Sue described her sugar cravings as significantly diminished. Over the next few weeks, we worked on a few more refinements to her diet, substituting fast-digesting carbohydrates that act like sugar in the body for less processed options, and adding whole, nutrient-dense meals to her dinner routine from my Eat Happy Meal Plan, the weekly dinner plan of simple recipes that use nutrient-dense unprocessed foods. She happily commented on how full and satisfied she felt after these meals, and the lack of cravings she experienced when eating this way.

Sue was surprised at how quickly she was able to turn around a lifetime of sugar cravings with just these few changes. She also mentioned what she called a "disposition effect," meaning that eating whole and unprocessed foods had an impact on her mood, or disposition. She felt happier and more relaxed eating this way, which took her by surprise. Most importantly, Sue gained a sense of control. She continued to travel and entertain family and friends, and occasionally enjoyed some sweet treats on special occasions. However, she knew exactly what to do if her cravings started to act up again and no longer felt like a slave to sugar. Another perk: After ten-plus years Sue was able to reduce her acid reflux medicine.

Salt

Like sugar, the sodium in salt has negative health effects that are well understood; it contributes to high blood pressure, heart attacks, and strokes. The average American consumes over 3,400 mg of sodium daily, which is 1.5 times the tolerable upper intake level and over 2 times the recommended adequate intake level.

Most salt in the American diet is coming from processed and restaurant foods. Unlike sugar, I frequently tell clients not to worry about salting their foods when they're cooking at home, because when you transition to unprocessed foods that have no added salt, adding a little to boost flavor isn't usually a problem. Homemade foods would be terribly bland without a pinch of salt. Of course, if you have high blood pressure or have been advised to watch your sodium intake by your doctor, you might have to be careful. But the vast majority of salt is coming from processed foods, and when you cut those down you'll naturally eliminate an enormous about of salt from your diet.

Salt, like sugar and certain fats, also has the wonderful advantage of being an adaptable taste. When you start to cut down, your taste buds will adapt. Cut down slowly over time, and after a month or two, if you try the foods you were used to consuming in the past, perhaps a canned soup or a soda, that food will taste uncomfortably salty or sweet. You won't want to continue eating it. This takes some time and patience, but it will happen.

Trans Fats

Trans fats, otherwise known as hydrogenated or partially hydrogenated oils, are man-made weapons of mass destruction in food form. They are created by adding a hydrogen atom (hence the "hydrogenated" part of the name) to vegetable oils. This does two things. It turns the liquid oil into a solid and prevents the oil from turning rancid for a nearly indefinite period of time. Food manufacturers absolutely loved this innovation, as it allowed them to make nice moist baked goods such as donuts and snack cakes that would essentially never spoil. That brand-name snack cake that's been sitting in the cupboard for 30 years and looks the same? That's thanks to trans fats, white flour, lots of sugar, and some additional preservatives for good measure. Trans fats are also used as fryer oils, shortenings and margarines, and even in some frozen ice-cream like desserts and drinks.

Originally trans fats were believed to be a more healthful alternative to butter and saturated fats. At one point the FDA estimated that trans fats were used in 95 percent of prepared cookies, 100 percent of crackers, and 80 percent of frozen breakfast products. Now we know that they are significantly more dangerous. They clog arteries, increase inflammation, and raise the bad LDL cholesterol that increases risks for heart disease, all significantly more than butter and natural animal fats. Health officials do not believe that any amount of trans fats is safe. They are banned in New York City, as well as a few others.

Due to pressure from consumers and public health organizations, trans fats have been significantly reduced, but they're still out there. And, there's a legal loop-hole to help manufacturers pull the wool over your eyes; if their products contain .5 grams or less per serving it can legally be listed as "0 grams" on the nutrition label. For this reason it's important to check the ingredients list and make sure that there are no hydrogenated or partially hydrogenated oils on the list.

Food Colorings, Preservatives, and the Rest

The other food additives that are extremely common and have known dangerous effects include various food colorings, artificial sweeteners, monosodium glutamate (MSG), which hides under many other names such as "yeast extract", sodium benzoate, and sodium nitrates and nitrites. Sadly foods that are heavily artificially colored are oftentimes targeted specifically at children, who are the most sensitive to their negative effects.

In a bit of good news, alternatives are popping up in stores that allow you to avoid these additives if you read labels carefully. Meats can be naturally preserved without nitrates and nitrites, although this usually involves a lot of salt. Some manufacturers are eliminating food colorings where they've traditionally been used (such as mint chocolate chip ice cream that's not green, but white), or there are plant-based natural options, such as using beet juice as a red coloring.

Food Detectives, Unite!

When I share this information at workshops, people are often bewildered that companies would knowingly put dangerous chemicals into our foods, including foods that are marketed specifically at children. It is important to keep in mind that food manufacturers and processors are large corporations, and their incentives for selling their products are very different than your incentives for eating. Any large corporation has an incredibly strong incentive to stay in business, to sell product and ensure profitability. Unfortunately for your health, the actions that are best for corporate profitability are all too often the worst for your health.

On the bright side, in a few instances of more extreme public pressure, some companies have been convinced to make changes. Trans fats were reduced across the US by 75 percent between 2005 and 2013, however the remaining 25 percent of trans fats that Americans consumed in 2013 was still a whopping 2 billion pounds. Under pressure from the food activist blogger "Food Babe", sandwich chain Subway committed to removing azodicarbonamide, an industrial chemical and known asthma trigger, from its breads.

These are a few positive examples, however I don't predict any time in the near future when all dangerous chemicals will be removed from foods. For the time being it's best to make a habit of reading food labels carefully.

Even better, and what I aim to teach you through the rest of this book, is to avoid foods that come with labels to begin with. If a label is attached it's a good sign it has been processed. Eating foods that contain only one ingredient (i.e. "rice" or "broccoli") is the best possible way to ensure that you're eating nutritionally dense, unadulterated real food.

How Do I Know If It's Highly Processed?
1. Are there unpronounceable or chemical-sounding ingredients on the food label?

2. Does the food last for unnatural amounts of time on a shelf?

3. Is the food an especially bright or strange color that doesn't exist in nature, at least for that food?

-3-
THE BASICS: WHAT TO EAT AND HOW TO COOK IT

Whole Foods Are Easy, Abundant and Delicious

Eating whole, unprocessed foods is easier than you'd think. The hardest thing is learning to recognize what these wonderful foods are. From there, learn a few simple preparation techniques and meals are a snap.

If you're not familiar with the kitchen and feel a little intimidated, it's ok. Many of my clients who haven't cooked much in the past are terrified to try new foods, but then quickly report back that they were delicious and easy.

The next few sections will describe a variety of foods and how to prepare them simply in their unprocessed forms. You'll see fool-proof charts of delicious unprocessed foods, how to best prepare them, and how long it will take.

If you're ready to transition your diet fully, that's great, but you don't need to go all or nothing. Aim to try a new food or two each week. You'll find your favorites, and after a few months have an entirely new repertoire of delicious go-to staple recipes.

Grains

Grains have gotten a bad rap lately, and it's too bad. Processed and refined grains deserve the bad press, but intact and unprocessed grains are loaded with nutrients, super easy to cook, and offer a lot of variety in tastes and textures to keep life interesting.

Most of my clients find whole grains to be very filling, and the nuttiness and chewiness of whole grains is particularly satisfying. New research even shows that the beneficial phytonutrient content of some grains can be higher than some fruits and vegetables.

Grains are best to eat in their whole and intact form. This ensures that their full amount of nutrients remains, and they'll digest slowly. Some grains, like corn (not sweet corn), need to be processed minimally to be edible. Corn is either ground into a meal and/ or soaked in lime water to enable digestion. Other forms of grains, such as bulgur or rolled oats, have been minimally processed to make their preparation faster. These processes may raise the glycemic index of the grains, but they are still relatively low versus more highly refined grains, and their nutrients are mostly in-tact.

General Spectrum of Grains

Worst (most processed)->	Better ->	Best (least processed)
White flour	Whole wheat flour, bulgur	Wheat berries
Barley, pearled	Barley, semi-pearled	Barley, hulled
Corn flour, germ removed	Corn flour, germ in-tact	Coarse corn meal (polenta)
Instant oats	Rolled oats	Steel-cut oats

All you really need to cook whole grains is a decent sized pot and some water. A fine-mesh sieve will make life easier as well.

General Instructions for Cooking Whole Grains:

1. Rinse grains and, if needed, soak overnight.
2. Drain the rinsing liquid and bring a pot of fresh water to a boil.
3. Add the grains to the water. If using the exact ratio of water to grains, cover and reduce to a simmer. If using extra water you can cover, partially cover, or just let the water boil and check it occasionally to make sure it doesn't get low.

4. Check the grains to see if they're done to your liking. There's some personal pref-
    erence here; some might like a grain softer, and others more al dente. Make it how
    you like it, then drain the cooking water.

A Few Additional Tips:

- For added flavor and nutrients grains can be cooked in stock. You can also add a
  quartered onion, a clove of garlic, herbs, or even juice.

- Some people like to make a big batch of grains once at the beginning of the week,
  then conveniently grab some as needed. This is a great strategy for an easy breakfast; add a little milk, fruit and nuts then quickly warm it up and you're good to go.

- Mechanical sorting is pretty good these days, but sometimes a small rock or a
  rogue grain of a different kind will make its way into the mix. It's a good idea to
  glance over your grains before adding them to the cooking water to make sure
  you're not about to cook anything undesirable. I almost never find anything, but
  occasionally there's a little something.

- You can improve the digestibility of many grains by adding a little acid, such as a
  squeeze of lemon or a little vinegar, to the soaking water.

- Rice has recently been found to have levels of inorganic arsenic that are causing
  some concern. While levels aren't high enough to recommend eliminating rice, I
  do recommend rinsing rice until the water runs clean, then using more cooking
  liquid than the minimum 2:1 ratio of water to rice, which can substantially reduce
  the arsenic left in the cooked grain. A ratio of 6:1 is recommended.

———————————— Libby's Story ————————————

Libby was a high-ranking professional in her mid-50s with a very health-conscious
diet when I met her. A long-time vegetarian, she was conscientious about what she ate and
practiced yoga and other forms of exercise regularly.

Despite her diet and lifestyle Libby wanted to feel better and decided to join my 12
Day Whole Foods Cleanse program. This program was designed to emphasize a clean
diet of whole, unprocessed foods for twelve days, which is enough time to feel the many
beneficial effects of a whole foods-based diet, but not so long to be daunting. Foods to

be eliminated included all processed sugars and flours, pre-packaged meals and snacks, and processed animal products. (Clean animal foods such as whole cuts of pasture-raised meats, fish and whole eggs were OK.) Because they are commonly undiagnosed food intolerances, the program also required eliminating gluten and dairy, as well as alcohol and caffeine which can disrupt natural energy reserves. Unlike many cleanses, this program was not a fast. Unlimited unprocessed foods were fair-game. (In fact eating to satisfaction was encouraged.)

I heard from Libby mid-way through the program with some interesting results. Below is the text from her email:

"Hi Alissa, I wanted to let you know how well I am doing. I have enjoyed the cleanse, and it's made me more mindful about eating and what to have on-hand at home and to take to work. I have lost 7 pounds, which was not my intention for doing the cleanse! The eczema on my thumbs has calmed down, which was very inflamed prior to the cleanse, and the skin condition on my back has cleared. I want to maintain eating this way."

After the cleanse was over Libby also mentioned the following benefits: improved energy, reduced food cravings, clearer sinuses, brighter eyes, improved digestion, improved mental clarity, elimination of the afternoon slump, and better sleep, and called the Cleanse an excellent experience.

Processed foods can infiltrate even the most conscientious of diets and some of the most heavily marketed "health foods" are in fact highly processed. The effects of removing processed foods from your diet can be so wide-ranging, it's fascinating to see what happens when you do.

If you're someone who enjoys the support of a group program such as a cleanse, I highly encourage trying my 12 Day Whole Foods Cleanse or another such program. When evaluating which program to try, I recommend selecting a program that emphasizes whole, unprocessed foods that you prepare for yourself and avoiding fasts or calorie controls; part of the beauty of eating unprocessed foods is that your self-regulation mechanisms begin to work again. I also recommend avoiding programs that seem to exist only to sell products such as shakes and supplements, which are in actuality the antithesis of unprocessed foods.

Should You Eat Gluten?

Gluten is a hot-button topic these days, with the validity of gluten-free diets hotly debated from various angles. Gluten is a protein that exists in wheat and its plant-based relatives, including rye, barley and spelt. Gluten-free diets require eliminating all foods containing this protein, which includes most breads, cereal products, and baked goods.

Certainly if you have celiac disease you must strictly avoid gluten. Non-celiac gluten intolerance is less well understood and there is no completely accurate test to detect it.

I have also witnessed many non-celiac clients, myself included, experience a wide-range of benefits from going gluten-free. Personally, I have been able to nearly eliminate migraines, sinus and allergy issues, and digestive problems by eliminating gluten and changing my diet to unprocessed foods. I have seen clients improve many of the same symptoms, as well as eliminate chronic joint and muscle pain, clear up skin conditions, and improve fibromyalgia, among other benefits.

For myself and many other individuals gluten-free diets have offered relief after years of discomfort, but for others they make no difference. Gluten is simply an issue for you or it's not. If it's not an issue for you you're lucky, because many gluten-containing grains are wonderfully healthy and convenient. Whole grain wheat, spelt, rye, and ancient grains like kamut and bulgur are wonderful foods to enjoy.

The only way to know for sure is to do an elimination diet. It must be done carefully to get clear results and I recommend that you work with a certified professional, such as a health coach, holistic nutritionist or registered dietician who can provide guidance and help you to interpret results. Additional information is provided at www.eathappynow. com as well.

Sam's Story

Sam was riddled with health problems when I first met her. She was in her early 40s and had experienced a significant amount of recent weight gain, however the problem that contributed most to her daily discomfort was her diagnosed fibromyalgia, which resulted in debilitating joint pain and stiffness. Despite a cocktail of steroid drugs, her pain on some days would reach a 9 or a 10 on a scale of 1-10 with 10 being the worst pain. She was also pre-diabetic, had high cholesterol, extreme fatigue, acid reflux, and the trifecta of gas, bloating and constipation on a regular basis.

Sam had been tested for celiac disease, which came back negative. However, due to her digestive symptoms, I suggested eliminating it from her diet for a couple of weeks. Sam had tried this before, but after a discussion about hidden gluten in processed foods, she realized she may not have eliminated all gluten sources. Spice mixes, which can contain various forms of gluten, and chicken, beef and vegetable stocks, which frequently contain wheat proteins as a thickener, were ingredients that were used frequently in her household. She cleaned out her cupboards and began a completely clean gluten-free diet.

The next time I saw Sam, about two weeks later, she was positively incredulous. Her joint pain and swelling was nearly gone; a 1 on the scale of 1-10. Her digestion had improved remarkably, and she was sleeping better. None of the medications she had been on over the past ten years had come close to resolving her symptoms as effectively as the gluten elimination. She maintained her gluten-free diet, and the positive results continued during the time we worked together.

I wished I could explain better to Sam how gluten sensitivity works on a biological level, but the reality is that even the world's best experts don't understand it that well, at least not yet. I have seen enough non-celiac gluten sensitivity in my clients to know that it's very real and that the only way to test for it is to strictly eliminate all gluten sources for a few weeks to see what happens.

It is best to work with an expert who can guide you on how to eliminate all gluten sources, including those that are hidden. Such an elimination diet may also require eliminating other common triggers at the same time, and will work best if you eat a clean and unprocessed diet throughout the elimination. You could, for example, eat nothing but gluten-free potato chips on your elimination diet, but that probably isn't going to be an accurate read of gluten sensitivity, because you'll likely feel awful just from eating all those potato chips.

Vegetables

Vegetables are incredibly powerful foods, and if you eat more of them they can transform your health.

That said, I always tell my clients that there is no one food I will ever force you to eat; this is even true of vegetables. There are so many delicious, widely available vegetables, that even if you don't like broccoli, or carrots, or whatever, I'm confident that you'll find a variety of vegetables that you do enjoy, especially when you learn simple ways to prepare them that enhance their flavor and maintain a texture that you enjoy.

Many non-vegetable eaters have bad memories of growing up with mushy canned or frozen vegetables with or without funky processed sauces that were obligatorily choked down. Vegetables don't have to be this way. We have more access to a huge variety of fresh vegetables than ever, and with the right kind of light preparation, these vegetables are truly delicious.

Instead of planning meals around animals proteins, such as chicken or beef, I suggest planning meals around your vegetables. Cultures with the best health and longest longevity, such as the traditional Mediterranean and Okinowan diets, eat this way. Start with what's in season and build your plate around that. I also recommend eating two servings of leafy green vegetables every day; the flush of nutrients you will be adding to your body will literally give it new life and energy.

Here's an overview of vegetables to look for and start enjoying:

Cruciferous Vegetables (The Cabbage Family)

I frequently give my clients a bunch of kale or another cruciferous vegetable to start eating right away and on a regular basis. A very common sentiment that I hear shortly after is, "maybe it's just mental, but I just feel better." I hear this response so often that I'm no longer surprised by this response.

The cabbage family includes some of the most nutrient-dense super foods in the supermarket. They contain sulfur-based compounds called glucosinolates that are known to have anticancer, heart-protective, and anti-inflammatory effects. Included in this family are kale, collard greens, mustard greens, Brussels sprouts, various cabbages, broccoli, cauliflower, kohlrabi, bok choy, arugula, and radishes among others. Kale is one of the densest in nutrients; as well as being high in glucosinolates and other antioxidants, a serving of kale has more calcium than six ounces of milk, and it's also extremely high in vitamins A, K and C.

Eating these foods daily, or at least several times per week, is one of the best things you can do for your body. When I hand my clients a bunch of fresh kale I'm usually excited for them to report back, and honestly I can't remember a single client who didn't enjoy it. While many of them were surprised at how much they enjoyed such a deep green leafy food, I've come to expect this response. Even better, clients feel the impact of these powerful foods within a few days to a week.

The key to enjoying kale is to 1) use the freshest kale possible, if it's old it will taste bitter and 2) not overcook it. Raw kale blends deliciously into smoothies and it develops a deep and almost nutty flavor when lightly steamed. Drizzle your steamed vegetables with a little sesame oil or extra virgin olive oil and sprinkle with sea salt.

Other Leafy Greens (Spinach and Lettuces)

Spinach and other leafy greens in the same family, including beet greens and Swiss chard, are high in antioxidants, vitamins and minerals, including vitamins A, K, folate, magnesium, iron and calcium among others. Spinach actually has more iron gram for gram than beef.

The most nutrient dense lettuces are those that are darkly colored, including reds, browns, and dark greens. Loose salad green mixes, romaine, and many varieties of heirloom lettuces are fun to experiment with. Unlike other leafy greens, iceberg is sadly lacking in nutrients; it's a nice source of water, but not much else.

Spinach and salad greens are usually enjoyed most when raw or very lightly cooked.

Onions, Garlic and Leeks (The Allium Family)

Garlic, onions, leeks, shallots, scallions, chives, and other relatives are practically as useful as medicine as they are as food, and they've been used historically in many cultures to do everything from prevent colds and flus to serve as poultices for wounds. When I feel a cold coming on, I smash a couple cloves of garlic and eat them daily for a few days (with food, to tolerate the spice). This might sound nutty, but there's solid science behind it.

Allicin, the main active ingredient in garlic, is a powerful antibiotic and has antiviral, antifungal, and anticancer properties as well. Quercetin is the main antioxidant in onions, and it increases with most cooking methods.

These vegetables are rarely the centerpiece of a meal, save for French onion soup perhaps, but they make just about everything they're used in taste better. Use them daily as a base for soups, sautés, salads, roasts, etc, and you'll be giving yourself a daily infusion of powerful medicine as well as kicking up the flavor in your dishes.

Root Vegetables

Sweet potatoes, russet and new potatoes, carrots, beets, rutabagas, parsnips, turnips, celeriac, and radishes are some of the diverse vegetables in this category. Many of these vegetables are extremely beautiful; they come in dramatic shades of purple, crimson, yellow and orange, and some have interesting color patterns. Their tastes vary from sweet to spicy, and their deep colors indicate their high levels of antioxidants.

The standard American diet is very high in processed white potatoes which have been nutritionally incapacitated. Whole russet potatoes can be a great and convenient food when eaten with their skins, which contain most of the nutrients. I suggest having some fun exploring other root vegetables, which can be a filling, satisfying, and beautiful way to fill your plate.

Mushrooms

Because mushrooms are so low in calories, we almost forget about them as a valuable food source. What they lack in calories they make up for in nutrients. What is most fascinating about mushrooms is that they contain chemicals that actually boost the immune system. Medicinal mushrooms have been used for thousands of years in Traditional Chinese Medicine (TCM), and even your standard white button mushroom is high in immune-boosting compounds.

Edible mushroom varieties include our common white button and portabello mushrooms, as well as shiitakes, oysters, criminis, and a variety of wild mushrooms. Most of these mushrooms need to be cooked to develop the nutritious compounds in them, and in fact our common button mushrooms should not be eaten raw due to some natural compounds that can have negative health effects. (These disappear once cooked.)

Other Veggies

Other vegetables, or foods we eat like vegetables, include tomatoes, asparagus, string beans, snap peas, peppers, artichokes, and others.

How to Simply Cook Your Vegetables, General Rules of Thumb

One of the wonderful things about cooking for yourself is that you can prepare your foods exactly how you like them. You're unique. No one will like things exactly as you do. I like my kale steamed or in smoothies, my Swiss chard sautéed with garlic, and root vegetables roasted with herbs. You might like the same, but you also might have different preferences, and that's ok.

Have fun trying new things, but when trying out a new vegetable I encourage you to go with something simple to start. Then you'll be able to add flavors and complexity as you see fit.

Cooked or Raw?

Many people assume that raw vegetables are the healthiest form. That's not always true. While some nutrients, such as Vitamin C, are heat-sensitive and are reduced with cooking, others such as certain anti-oxidants are made more bio-available with heat. Lycopene, the powerful antioxidant in tomatoes, is up to ten times higher in tomato paste, which has been cooked for long periods of time. In addition, some people will have difficulty digesting certain raw vegetables, but cooking makes them much easier on the digestive system. Enjoy a variety of fresh and lightly cooked vegetables to get a well-rounded assortment of nutrients.

Here are a few rules of thumb when preparing vegetables:

1. Many vegetables skins are edible and high in nutrients. Try scrubbing and leaving the skins on, which will also save you time. This is possible for most root vegetables, including potatoes, sweet potatoes, and carrots. It's nice to buy organic if possible, which alleviates any concerns about chemical residue on the skin surface.

2. In most cases, especially with green vegetables, light cooking so that the vegetable is still crisp-tender preserves most of its nutrients.

3. Steaming is preferable to boiling, which leaches nutrients into the cooking water. If you're preparing a soup or stew it's OK, as you'll get those nutrients back.

General Instructions for Cooking Vegetables

Steaming

If there is one preparation method to go to by default, this is it. It's the fastest and generally most nutritious way to prepare vegetables. Steaming also has the easiest clean-up so it wins across the board. You can steam vegetables in a medium pot with a tight-fitting lid simply by adding 1/2 inch of water to the bottom. Heat up the water to a simmer, add the vegetables and a lid and cook until just tender. For many vegetables this happens quite quickly, in about one to four minutes. You may need to toss the vegetables once for even cooking. One exception is whole artichokes, which need to steam for a good 45 minutes before they're ready to eat. (They are, btw, well worth the wait.)

You can also invest about $9 in a metal steaming tray. These fold up and down to accommodate different sized pots and hold the vegetables up and out of the water. Because the vegetables aren't sitting in the actual water, they'll lose fewer nutrients to the cooking liquid, so it's a nice tool to have. I like to finish off steamed vegetables with a little extra virgin olive oil and some sea salt or garlic salt. The oil adds flavor and improves absorption of many fat-soluble nutrients, so enjoy it.

Sautéing

Some vegetables taste better sautéed than steamed, but again it's all subject to personal preference. I find that onions, mushrooms, certain greens like spinach and Swiss chard, and crunchy vegetables like peppers taste especially great after a quick sauté.

To sauté vegetables you'll need a large sauté or fry pan and a little oil. Keep the heat low to medium-low so that your oil doesn't smoke. (This makes it taste bad and also creates dangerous chemicals.) Add the oil to the pan, and when it's warm add your vegetables. Move the vegetables around the pan until they're exactly how you like them. You can add a little garlic to the warm oil either at the beginning or end of the sauté, depending on how spicy you like your garlic. The longer you cook it, the milder it will become. Season everything with a little sea salt and black pepper while it's cooking. Most vegetables will sauté in 3-5 minutes, and mushrooms can take a little longer at 8-10.

Stir-fried dishes that include many ingredients, for example snap peas, onions, peppers, and shrimp, are a simple and fast way to create a one-dish meal. Just add the ingredients that need to cook the longest first, and vice versa. In this example, because shrimp usually cook in only 60 seconds, they should be added last.

Roasting

I do a lot of roasting in the winter, piling mounds of vegetables onto large baking sheets with a little oil, some salt and pepper, a few cloves of garlic, and maybe some dried herbs. It's quick and efficient, and clean up is especially easy if you use parchment paper or a silicon mat to line your baking sheet.

Roasting has a special ability to develop and concentrate sweetness in vegetables. One of my favorite winter dishes is to take a variety of root vegetables, cut them into 2-inch chunks, and roast them all together. They'll become sweet and caramelized. Brussels sprouts, onions, broccoli, root vegetables, asparagus, and even tomatoes take very well to roasting.

Most vegetables roast well between 375 and 400 degrees. Lightly coat your vegetables in a good-quality oil such as extra virgin olive oil or grapeseed oil and a sprinkling of salt and pepper. Add dried herbs or garlic as you like. Spread them single layer in a shallow dish. This is important, because if they're not single-layer, they'll steam themselves and won't develop a nice crispiness. Cooking time can vary from 20 to 45 minutes for most vegetables and will depend on the size. You'll likely want to toss the vegetables once to promote even browning. You'll know they're done when a sharp knife goes into and out of the vegetable easily, indicating it's tender.

Baking

The only vegetables that I generally bake in their entirety are whole potatoes and sweet potatoes. There is nothing easier than scrubbing a sweet potato or russet potato for a few seconds, pricking it once or twice with a sharp knife, and popping it in the oven on 400 degrees for 45 minutes to an hour. No foil or oil rubs are needed.

The pricking step is important; otherwise steam can build up in the potato and cause it to explode. Also, if baking sweet potatoes, it's a good idea to place some foil on a baking sheet underneath to catch drippings. Sweet potatoes will develop a sticky syrup that will leak from the potato while it cooks. It's an indication of the sweet deliciousness inside, but it's a major pain to scrub out of an oven.

Boiling

Like steaming, virtually any vegetable can be boiled until it's ready to eat. However, it's not a recommended cooking method for most vegetables because in so many instances a large percentage of the nutrients will leach into the water. If soups or stews are the end result, then it's OK; you'll get them back in the broth. If you just want to cook the vegetable then steaming is a better method. It's also faster and requires less time to bring the water to a boil.

Beans, Peas and Lentils

Beans, peas and lentils, also known as legumes, are the great forgotten foods of the American diet. Large parts of the world survive on these foods as staples, and they provide a robust array of flavors and textures, as well as nutrients and health benefits. Thanks to their high glutamate content, which gives them a "meaty" umami flavor, legumes provide a similar satisfaction to meat and make a great base for vegetarian meals. They're equally useful for adding to a wide variety of dishes, including salads, curries, and soups that may or may not contain meat.

Studies show that people who eat legumes on a regular basis have lower rates of cancer, heart disease, diabetes, obesity, and digestive diseases. Legumes are high in fiber, protein, and a variety of vitamins and minerals including iron, folate, and copper, among others, but they're also surprisingly high in antioxidants. Lentils, black beans, and red kidney beans actually have more antioxidants per serving than blueberries, with lentils having the most. This is a surprise for the very plain-looking lentil, but great news, because lentils are relatively fast to cook, don't require soaking, and are extremely versatile. Lentils are my favorite go-to quick dinner when I don't have anything planned and need something quick. (See my Lentil and Potato Curry with Coconut Milk recipe in the Recipe section).

The Magical Fruit

Some people veer away from beans because they're concerned about gas. That lovely childhood song ("beans, beans the magical fruit, the more you eat the more you toot!") has indoctrinated too many of us into believing that we'll suffer greatly if we indulge in the magical fruit. I actually do not find in my practice that beans are a great contributor to gas or bloating. More likely culprits are processed sugar and flours as well as intolerances to dairy and wheat or gluten.

Some people lack a digestive enzyme that breaks down the carbohydrate in beans. If you're one of these people, you may wish to eat fewer of the beans that are most likely to cause gas, including lima beans, pigeon beans, kidney beans, and green split peas. Thankfully my favorite, lentils, are low on this list. We all have our own unique threshold for various foods; keep in mind you're much less likely to have symptoms after one serving than if you eat the same thing three meals in a row.

There are easy steps you can and should take to make your legumes as digestible as possible. Simply soaking dried beans overnight in water, or doing a "quick soak" of boiling beans for twenty minutes and then letting them sit for one to two hours and then discarding the soaking liquid, will break down many of the carbohydrates that can cause gas. And, there's always Beano or a similar digestive enzyme you can buy from the store, which provides that missing enzyme to people who need it.

Soaking has other advantages, too, as it lowers the amount of "antinutrients" in some beans. Phytic acid and lectins, two of the more common antinutrients, bind to nutrients and prevent them from being absorbed by the body. They're almost entirely disabled by soaking and cooking, but it is a good reason to make sure that your beans are fully cooked when you eat them. There are some case studies of individuals becoming acutely ill from eating under-cooked beans (very rare though).

Dried versus Canned

Good news: Both dried legumes and canned are excellent choices. Dried beans are available in more varieties than canned, and they're extremely inexpensive. In fact, I feel they're the least expensive health foods in the world, and when people talk about the high price of eating healthfully I tend to talk excitedly about beans and brown rice. If you think ahead, you can cook dried beans in large quantities and store them in glass pint jars packed with a little of their cooking liquid in your freezer. Glass jars made for canning have been treated to withstand extreme temperatures, and are one of the most stable materials in which to store food.

Canned beans are undeniably convenient. Unlike fruits and vegetables, beans don't lose substantial amounts of nutrients when they're canned. In fact, some of their phytonutrients are increased. I like to think of canned beans as a wonderful fast-food option. This is the good kind of processed food, as long as they don't have anything funky added to them. Hardly a thing needs to be done to them to whip up a delicious and nutritious soup, salad or dip. Some legumes, such as lentils and split peas, which don't require soaking, aren't oftentimes available in cans, because there's not a huge benefit in convenience.

The one concern with canned foods in general is bisphenol A (BPA), a chemical used in the epoxy lining of the lids. BPA is known to act as an endocrine disruptor by acting like hormone in the body. There is growing concern about its link to brain and behavior problems, cancer, heart problems, and diabetes and obesity. Children who are developing and hormonally sensitive are at highest risk of being affected.

Many food manufacturers are actively looking into alternatives to BPA to use in their canned foods. Some manufacturers are beginning to offer more foods in cartons or glass that have no need for BPA. If your grocery store has these available, they're excellent options.

BPA is more likely to leach into acidic liquids such as tomatoes, and one study found that the highest BPA levels were in canned green beans, in which some acid is usually added to maintain the beans' color. Canned legumes aren't particularly acidic, so I don't feel it's critical to avoid them, and the benefits likely outweigh the risks. However, especially if you are pregnant or have very young kids, it might be worth it to pay a little more for alternative packing if it's available.

Simple Instructions for Cooking Dried Legumes

1. Soak dried legumes, if needed:
    1.a. Long soak method: Cover beans with a several inches of fresh water and let them sit on the counter overnight or for 8 hours. Then drain the soaking liquid.
    1.b. Quick soak method: Cover beans with a several inches of fresh water in a large pot and bring to a boil. Boil on high for 20 minutes then turn off the stove, cover and let them sit in the hot water for 1-2 hours. Drain soaking liquid.
2. Boil a large pot of fresh water and simmer legumes until tender. You could also directly add soaked legumes, or those that don't need to be soaked, to soups or stews that need to cook for the duration of the expected cooking time. Easy Peasy.

A Few Other Beany Tips

- A few smaller beans, like adzuki beans, mung beans and black-eyed peas don't need to be soaked, although they can be. They will be slightly more digestible and will cook faster if you do soak them.
- Don't add salt until the beans are nearly done cooking; adding it early can make beans tough.
- Cooked beans can be stored in the freezer with a little cooking liquid for several months. I like to make big batches, then freeze in glass canning jars with wide-mouth lids, which makes them easy to get out of the jar even if they aren't completely thawed.

- Once beans are done cooking, if you let them sit in the cooking water for an extra hour they'll plump up and their antioxidant level will increase. This isn't necessary for lentils or split peas.

- The fresher the beans are, the faster they'll cook. If your beans have been soaked and seem to be taking an eternity to cook, they're likely just old. It doesn't mean they're bad, but buying them from a store or market with more turnover will be more convenient for you.

- A health food store or farmer's market may have many kinds of heirloom beans. Have fun finding the tastes and textures that you enjoy the most.

Legume Cooking Times

Legume	Suggested Uses	Soak?
Adzuki	45-90 minutes	Can, not necessary
Black Beans	60-90 minutes	Y
Black-Eyed Peas	45-60 minutes	Can, not necessary
Cannellini	60-90 minutes	Y
Chickpeas /Garbanzo	120-160 minutes	Y
Great Northern	90-120 minutes	Y
Kidney	60-90 minutes	Y
Lentils, Green	25-35 minutes	N
Lentils, Red	20-25 minutes	N
Lentils, Black/Beluga	20-25 minutes	N
Lima Beans	60-90 minutes	Y
Mung Beans	45-60 min	N
Navy Beans	60-90 minutes	Y
Pinto Beans	60-90 minutes	Y
Split Peas, green or yellow	45-90 minutes	N

Meats, Eggs and Fish

Before the Store

Before humans began domesticating animals, hunter-gatherers lived on wild game such as deer, bison, rabbits, wild turkey, etc, that foraged for food. These animals ate their wild diets of whatever was natural to them, whether it was other animals, plants, or insects. These days most of our meat and eggs, and increasingly fish, come from large commercial-scale farms that manage the entire life cycle of the animals. What these animals eat, including their nutrition and various drugs and chemicals, affects what exactly is in their flesh.

Most of our commercially raised animals are fed corn and soybeans as well as cocktails of antibiotics and hormones that reduce costs and make the animals grow faster, reducing their time to market. Chickens, turkeys and hogs, until recently, were commonly fed arsenic, a known carcinogen, for the same reasons. This practice is still legal for turkeys.

These practices are significant for a few reasons. The feed animals eat affects the nutrients that transfer through to their meat, milk and eggs. Commercially raised beef, milk, and farmed salmon, for example, have lower levels of omega-3 fatty acids, the extremely healthful and anti-inflammatory fat that most Americans aren't getting enough of. Secondly, the chemicals that are fed to animals transfer through to their products as well, essentially making them an ingredient in our food. Because they're part of the farming process, just like pesticides and fungicides, they do not need to be listed on the label. Most Americans have no idea that, for decades, their chicken contained arsenic.

Increasing awareness about these issues is leading more and more consumers to look for alternatives, and manufacturers are providing them. Buying organic products ensures that many of the hormones and chemicals used in conventional products are not used. "Grass-fed" beef and milk designates that cows were primarily pasture-raised, which is their traditional diet. For poultry and pork the terminology isn't yet as well regulated, but pasture-raised ensures that the animals at least had some ability to forage for their natural foods.

The best way to know what your animals have eaten and how they were raised is to know your farmer. Most farmers are more than happy to tell you about their practices, and in general small-scale farms are more judicious about their practices because they also consume their products. Your taste buds will thank you also; most people taste a noticeable difference between commercial and small-farm foods, with the smaller farm creating richer, tastier flavors.

In the Aisle

Meat

Unlike processed meats, including sausages, bacon, ham, lunch meats, patties and burgers of various kinds, and even plain ground meats (pink slime, anyone?), unprocessed meats have been minimally changed from how they exist on an animal. They include whole forms and cuts, including:

Chicken and Turkey: Whole, quartered, legs, breasts, thighs

Beef: Various steaks and roasts, stew meat cuts

Pork: Various roasts, pork chops, ribs

Sausage and the Rest: Bacon, sausages, and other processed meats aren't always bad. If they're coming from a butcher you know and trust, or a local farm that uses ingredients conscientiously, you can avoid the dangerous additives and processing ingredients that are used on a large commercial scale. Ingredients you want to avoid include sodium nitrates and nitrates, which are among the most cancer-causing of all food additives, and monosodium glutamate, which is used in spice mixes.

Ground Meats: I also recommend being careful about the ground meats that you buy. Recently the news about "pink slime" went mainstream and much of the public was horrified to learn that up to 25 percent of their ground beef was actually this highly processed meat additive. Pink slime is created when scrap meat, cartilage and connective tissues are mechanically processed with heat, and put through a centrifuge to create a kind of liquid meat. This meat is then processed with either ammonium hydroxide or citric acid to kill pathogens. Because the chemicals used are in the manufacturing process, they do not need to be listed on the food label. Foods treated with ammonium hydroxide are illegal in some countries, including Canada.

Ground meats that are made from whole cuts are relatively unprocessed and a good, affordable source of meat. However, there aren't any laws currently requiring pink slime to be labeled, and any labeling taking place is at the will of the manufacturer.

Fish: Whole fish and filets, domestic shrimp and shellfish.

Eggs: Eggs are a wonderful and widely available unprocessed food source. I frequently recommend that travelers look for hard-boiled eggs in airports, as they're often one of the least processed options available and are very satisfying. Don't be afraid to eat the whole egg. The yolk contains all of the nutrients, and the myth that eating eggs raises dietary cholesterol has been debunked. Eating processed sugars, flours, and trans fats are much more likely to raise cholesterol than whole eggs.

General Instructions for Cooking Whole Meats and Cuts

The most important factor in cooking animal proteins is to get them to the right internal temperature so that they're safe to eat. The best way to do this is to use a meat thermometer inserted into the center of the deepest part of boneless cuts, and the deepest part near the bone of cuts that contain bones (bones heat more slowly, so the meat closest to them tends to cook the most slowly).

Because grass-fed and naturally pastured meats tend to have fewer dangerous pathogens than commercially raised meats, there are two sets of recommended internal temperatures, one from the USDA, and one from Eatwild.com which has a wealth of information on naturally-raised meats (see Resources).

Animal Protein Temperature Guide

Meat	Grass-fed Meat	USDA Recommended Temp
Beef and Bison	120-140F	145-170F
Ground Meat	160F	160F
Veal	125-155F	145-170F
Lamb and Goat	120-145F	145-170F
Pork	145-160F	145-170F
Chicken (unstuffed)	165F	165F
Turkey	165F	165F

Other Helpful Tips

- Ask your butcher/fish monger for suggestions on how to cook cuts or products if you're not sure. They'll give you great ideas on easy and tasty ways to prepare their products.
- Once your meats are thawed it's best to use them within a couple days; fresh fish should be eaten within 2-3 days, but if in doubt, ask when you're buying.
- How long at the specified temperature.
- Resting and redistributing juices.

Fish

High quality fish can actually be eaten raw and is delicious, hence the popularity of sushi. If you like your fish more rare, ask your fish monger which varieties he or she would recommend. For most fish, it's relatively easy to see when it's cooked through, as the flesh will have turned from firm to flaky, and in pink fishes like wild salmon from bright pink or red to a lighter color. Salmon and tuna are frequently enjoyed more rare in the middle.

Eggs

Official government recommendations are to cook eggs until their whites and yolks are firm, at 160 degrees, in order to kill salmonella which can exist on the outsides of shells as well as penetrate them. Many people enjoy their egg yolks on the runny side. Eggs from small farms are less likely to be contaminated from salmonella, so I feel comfortable eating medium-soft and slightly runny eggs from these sources. The risk of salmonella, even from commercial farms, is relatively low and pasteurized eggs are available, so use your best judgment when preparing eggs.

Cooking methods

Baking and Roasting

Any cut of meat, fish, and even eggs can be baked or roasted until they are cooked through, and a medium-large roasting pan such as a 13 x 9 inch dish will get a lot of use in your kitchen. Seasonings can be as simple as a rub of extra virgin olive oil and sprinkle of salt and pepper. Like steaming is my go-to preparation method for cooking vegetables, baking is my go-to technique for meats and fish. All you need to do is grease your pan lightly with oil or butter, place your cut of meat or fish in the pan, add whatever seasoning you like, and cook until the right temperature is reached. Baking eggs can be super easy and very cute, especially if you have individual baking dishes, just be sure to grease whatever dish you put them in so they'll slide out easily.

Stove Top (Sautéing and Frying)

Stove-top preparations simply involve a sauté or fry pan on a hot stove and usually a little fat or liquid to prevent sticking. Stove-top methods generally work better for thinner cuts of meats and fish that will cook more quickly. Again, seasoning can be as simple as a little olive oil with salt and pepper, and you can add flavors as you like.

Cooking in Liquids (Boiling, Poaching, Stewing)

All of the above methods are simply ways to cook in liquids. Cooking in liquids has the advantage of keeping foods moist, and it works well for some tougher cuts if they're allowed to cook on a low boil (simmer) over a long period of time. Usually animal proteins aren't cooked in plain water, but rather liquids that provide flavor, such as stocks, broths, wine, and the juices that emerge from vegetables or even fruit.

Misc; Cookware

Dairy

Dairy is a controversial food, for good reason. On the one hand, it's a good source of certain nutrients, including calcium. We've all been told for so many years to eat many servings of dairy per day in order to build strong bones.

On the other hand dairy has many negatives which are not as well publicized. Many people are intolerant to dairy, either via lactose intolerance or intolerances or allergies to the proteins. Because it's one of the foods that most people eat daily, it's surprisingly common for a dairy intolerant person to be completely unaware of the association between eating dairy and their symptoms.

On a wider scale, dairy exacerbates the body's allergic response and can therefore make other allergies worse, can be inflammatory, and large consumption of dairy is correlated with an increased risk of hormone-driven cancers such as breast and prostate cancer. Whether it's a good idea for you to eat dairy is largely based on your body and your health history.

One thing is certain. Many dairy products have become very, very processed. Many yogurts, which are almost universally believed to be health foods, have so much sugar and other additives, that they are simply glorified and highly processed desserts. Some eight-ounce yogurts have more sugar in them than twelve-ounce sodas. Many commercial yogurts don't even include live probiotics, as they've been processed in such a way that kills the beneficial bacteria. Probiotics are the beneficial bacteria that can improve digestion and immune system function. They're the reason many people eat yogurt to begin with. This is a food example of a wolf in sheep's clothing.

Use the same rules as other foods to evaluate whether dairy products are a minimally processed food. What has been added/taken away? Has the form of the food been unusually manipulated? Is it a crazy color? If any warning bells go off, avoid it.

If you eat dairy, I recommend whole milk or whole milk plain yogurt which has been naturally cultivated and still contains live active probiotics. These are the least processed dairy options available and have some legitimate health benefits.

Snacks

I get so many questions about good snack options. First and foremost; you shouldn't be starving all of the time and in desperate need of snacks. This is a sure sign that you need to eat more during your meal. Transitioning to unprocessed foods will mean that you likely need to increase your portion sizes. This is what I mean by eating more food. Unprocessed foods are less calorie dense and your serving sizes will likely need to be larger.

If you are hungry all of the time I recommend that you make your meals more satisfying by 1) eating more or 2) eating more fat. Fat is super satisfying. Good fats like extra virgin olive oil, avocados, and nuts will really help to balance your blood sugar and keep you happy. Studies show that people who eat lots of nuts weight less, so don't be afraid of them.

That said, it's normal to need to eat every three to four hours, even with satisfying whole-foods based meals. So if you eat lunch at noon and dinner at 7 p.m., a snack in-between is OK but you still shouldn't feel starving. I recommend:

- Nuts
- Seeds
- Nut and seed butters
- Dried fruits that haven't had sugar added
- Fresh fruits and vegetables
- Bean dips such as hummus
- Really anything else that's a real food

Nuts, seeds, and dried or fresh fruits are undeniably convenient. They travel and store well, don't need to be refrigerated, and will give you long lasting energy to make it to your next meal.

Cookware

Good cookware will last a lifetime, so I find it makes more sense to start with just a couple important pieces and add quality ones as you can. Here are a couple of essentials:

1. **A good knife**: A good chef's knife is all you need to do about 95 percent of your chopping. It's worth the investment, you might actually enjoy chopping your vegetables, and you're less likely to cut yourself. Counter-intuitive for a sharper tool, but true.

2. **A large pot with lid:** Use for soups, stews, steaming vegetables, stocks, etc. If you could only have one pot or pan in your kitchen, this is what I'd recommend. In a

pinch you could actually do everything you need in this, including sauté, steam and boil. A good quality pot or pan will be made of substantial materials that distribute heat evenly across the bottom surface, which prevents foods on the inside from burning. This means you can simmer soups and sauces for hours if you want to, and your other foods will cook evenly.

3. **A large sauté pan with a lid**: If you can swing it, a sauté pan with a lid is super convenient. You can sauté vegetables, quickly steam or boil vegetables and legumes, and even sear or braise meats.

4. **A small to medium non-stick pan**: I use non-stick cookware for pretty much one thing: eggs. If you don't like eggs then I wouldn't even bother, but I make eggs frequently so my non-stick pan gets a lot of use. Your average non-stick coatings are made up of chemicals that have legitimate safety concerns. The most stable (i.e. safest) non-stick cookware available is actually ceramic.

5. **A large roasting pan/casserole dish**: Something close to a 13 x 9 inch pan that has deep enough sides for casseroles (2 1/2 to 3 inches) will get a lot of use and is very versatile. You can roast meats or vegetables, make lasagna, and even bake brownies in it.

I would also recommend a good pair of kitchen tongs and a silicon spatula and wood spoon or two. Silicon is a very heat resistant and stable material, so look for silicon parts instead of plastics for utensils that will be in direct contact with hot foods.

From these basics, you can expand your cookware collection to provide you with more convenience and fun while cooking. You may find that adding pots in a few different sizes allows you to get more done at once. Another pan that I use frequently is my cast-iron skillet. I love it for cooking burgers, searing meats, and even making pancakes. A well-seasoned cast-iron pan, which basically means it's been well-oiled and used regularly, develops a nice non-stick surface, just not quite non-stick enough for eggs.

- 4 -

WHOLE-FOODS RECIPES

INTRODUCTION

I'm so excited for you to begin preparing simple and delicious meals out of whole, unprocessed foods. I hope you'll be pleasantly surprised at the ease of preparation and the level of flavor and satisfaction that you get out of each meal.

Here are a few tips to keep in mind while preparing these meals:

1. **Have a plan:** Most of us are busy in our daily lives, and it is always helpful to have a plan. Many, although not all whole foods such as grains, dried legumes, and even meats, will require soaking or longer duration thawing, often just a few minutes the day before preparing a meal will ensure successful execution the fol¬lowing day.

2. **Consider a meal planning guide:** I have found meal planning to be such an important factor in the success of transitioning to unprocessed foods that I now publish a weekly meal plan called Eat Happy Meal Plan, which is available at www.eathappymealplan.com. It is extremely affordable, includes a wide variety of whole and unprocessed food ingredients, and provides all of the necessary planning steps to save you time and energy. There are also a variety of apps and tools that can help you save time with your own meal planning.

3. **Season to taste:** I rarely designate specific amounts of salt and pepper and rather suggest that you season to taste. Unless you have high blood pressure or other health concerns that are relevant to salt consumption, don't be afraid to add a little sea salt to your dishes if they seem bland, as this can truly be the difference between delicious and boring meals, especially if your taste buds are transitioning from a processed diet. It's more effective to add a little salt as you cook versus all at the end, because it coaxes more flavors out of the ingredients while they're developing. The total amount that you add on your own will almost certainly be less than what a food manufacturer would put in for you.

4. **Eat your leftovers**: I almost never buy foods specifically for lunch because I always have leftovers from dinner that pack up quite well. A good friend of mine packs her leftovers directly into individual-serving sized containers so that she can simply grab one on her way to work. You can also freeze leftovers in individual sized containers for days when you need a break from cooking.

Most vegetables preserve well once lightly steamed, so you can steam vegetables at the beginning of the week for easy munching or tossing into salads or other recipes throughout the week

SIMPLE STEAMED VEGGIES

Total Prep Time: 5-10 minutes
Active Time: 5 minutes
Serves: 4

Ingredients
1 lb veggies cut into bite-sized pieces (kale, green beans, broccoli, swiss chard, cauliflower, carrots, etc)
Extra virgin olive oil (EVOO)
Sea salt

Directions
You can use a steamer, steam basket insert, or simply a regular sauce pan with a tight-fitting lid to steam your vegetables.

Heat about ½ inch of water in whatever vessel you're using until it is simmering. Place veggies either directly in the pan or the steam basket and place the lid on. Most vegetables will steam in about 3-5 minutes. Asparagus cooks very quickly in 1-2 minutes, especially if it's very thin. Toss the vegetables once while in the pan to encourage even cooking (this may not be necessary with a steam basket). Check them and take them out when they're done to your liking. Drizzle with a little EVOO, sprinkle lightly with salt, then serve.

COOK'S NOTES

Garlic is a delicious and nutritious way to kick up any green vegetable. To get the most nutrients from your garlic crush or mince the clove, then let it sit for five to ten minutes before heating. This way the garlic's active ingredients will develop fully.

SIMPLE SAUTÉED GREENS WITH GARLIC

Total Prep Time: 10 minutes
Active Time: 10 minutes
Serves: 4

Ingredients
1 lb leafy greens (spinach, Swiss Chard, bok choy mustard greens, etc), rinsed and cut or torn into 2-3 inch pieces
3 cloves garlic, smashed and skins removed, or 3 teaspoons minced
Extra virgin olive oil (EVOO), sea salt, and freshly cracked black pepper
Optional add-ins: hot sauce or crushed red pepper, 2 teaspoons of lemon juice or balsamic vinegar
Extra virgin olive oil (EVOO), sea salt and black pepper

Directions
1. Heat a large drizzle of EVOO in your largest sauté pan over medium-low heat.
2. Add the greens and season them with a little salt and pepper. Toss them gently around the pan, increasing the heat if necessary, until they are evenly coated with the oil and begin to wilt, about 5 minutes. Add the garlic and continue to sauté until the greens are to your desired level of tenderness. If the pan is very full you can accelerate the wilting by adding a couple of tablespoons of water to the pan and placing a lid on top for 1-2 minutes (this causes steam which wilts the greens).
3. Be sure to taste the greens along the way and season them with salt and pepper as they're cooking to taste.

COOK'S 🥕 NOTES

If you wash and pat dry your salad greens when you bring them home from the grocery store you can save them in a plastic zip top bag and throw together an easy salad in minutes. The tiny bit of mustard in the salad dressing provides flavor and also helps the oil and vinegar emulsify.

SIMPLE GREEN SALAD

Total Prep Time: 5 minutes
Active Time: 5 minutes
Serves: 4

Ingredients
Vinegar (balsamic or red wine)
Sea salt and black pepper
5-7 ounces of your favorite greens (romaine, spinach, arugula, baby green mix, etc)
Chopped or sliced veggies if desired (carrots, celery, red onion, pepper, etc)
½ tsp Dijon mustard, optional
Extra virgin olive oil (EVOO), sea salt and fresh black pepper

Directions
1) Rinse greens and spin or pat dry (even bagged greens benefit from a rinse), put into a large bowl.
2) In a small condiment bowl, whisk together ¼ cup of olive oil (no need to measure, just eyeball) with 2 tablespoons of vinegar. Add mustard, salt and pepper, whisk again and drizzle over greens. Toss together. Add whatever veggies from your fridge you like.

COOK'S NOTES

ORANGE GLAZED SPINACH

Total Prep Time: 10 minutes
Active Time: 10 minutes
Serves: 4

Ingredients

1 lb fresh spinach

Juice from 1 large naval orange, or other good juicing orange

Extra virgin olive oil (EVOO), sea salt, freshly cracked black pepper

Directions

1. Place a large fry pan over medium heat. Add the juice from the orange and bring to a simmer. Let it reduce by about 1/3, then add the spinach.

2. Sauté the spinach in the orange juice while stirring regularly to help the spinach wilt. Season with a little salt and pepper. When the spinach is nearly wilted to your liking add about a tablespoon of EVOO to finish the spinach, toss until it's well combined with the orange juice, then turn off the heat. Serve immediately.

COOK'S NOTES

ROASTED BRUSSELS SPROUTS AND CAULIFLOWER

Total Prep Time: 40 minutes
Active Time: 5 minutes
Serves: 4

Ingredients

1 lb Brussels sprouts, rinsed and any damaged outer leaves removed
I head cauliflower, cut into 1-2 inch florets and rinsed
1 head garlic, cloves separated and skins removed (the easiest way to do this is to smash the cloves so that the skins are loosened)
Extra virgin olive oil (EVOO), sea salt, freshly cracked black pepper

Directions

1. Pre-heat the oven to 400 degrees and position a rack in the middle of your oven.
2. If any Brussels sprouts or cauliflower florets are especially large cut them in half through the core so that the Brussels sprouts will cook evenly.
3. Toss the vegetables and garlic with a large drizzle of EVOO and a generous pinch of sea salt and fresh black pepper. Arrange in a single-layer on a large baking sheet and roast until tender, about 35 minutes. Toss them with a spatula half way through cooking to ensure even baking.

COOK'S NOTES

GREEN BEAN FRIES

Total Prep Time: 30 minutes
Active Time: 5 minutes
Serves: 4

Ingredients
1 bag frozen green beans or 1 lb fresh green beans, tough ends trimmed
Extra virgin olive oil (EVOO), sea salt, freshly cracked black pepper

Directions
Pre-heat the oven to 400 degrees. Toss the green beans with 2 tablespoons of EVOO and lots of sea salt and black pepper. Spread them in a single layer on a baking sheet (try using a silicon mat for extra-easy clean-up) and bake for 25-30 minutes for frozen green beans or 15-20 minutes for fresh, until crispy, tossing once about 2/3 of the way through cooking time.

COOK'S NOTES

This salad is refreshing, tart and tangy, and sweet. It's one of the most delicious ways I know to use super affordable and nutritious cabbage.

CABBAGE AND APPLE SALAD WITH CHERRIES AND PECANS

Total Prep Time: 25 minutes
Active Time: 15 minutes
Serves: 4

Ingredients

1 cup pecans, toasted
2 tablespoons seasoned rice vinegar
1 tablespoon apple cider vinegar
1 teaspoon Dijon mustard
2 apples
2 tablespoons fresh lemon juice
½ red cabbage, thinly sliced (about 3 cups)
½ Napa, Savory or green cabbage, thinly sliced (about 3 cups)
3/4 cup dried tart cherries
Extra virgin olive oil (EVOO), sea salt and black pepper

Directions

1. Whisk vinegars, mustard and ¼ cup olive oil with salt and pepper to taste.
2. Toss the apples with the lemon juice (this will prevent browning), then put them into a bowl with the cabbage, cherries and pecans. Toss with the dressing and serve.

COOK'S NOTES

ARUGULA SALAD WITH STRAWBERRIES, WALNUTS AND AVOCADO

Total Prep Time: 20 minutes
Active Time: 10 minutes
Serves: 4

Ingredients
8 ounces arugula, chopped into bite-sized pieces if desired
2 cups strawberries, sliced or quartered and stems removed
2 ripe avocados, pits removed and sliced
½ cup walnuts, lightly toasted
3 tablespoons balsamic vinegar
¼ tsp Dijon mustard
½ tsp garlic powder
Extra virgin olive oil (EVOO), sea salt, freshly cracked black pepper

Directions
1. Whisk together the vinegar, Dijon mustard, garlic powder, 1/3 cup EVOO, and some salt and pepper.
2. Toss the dressing with the arugula, strawberries, avocados and pecans in a large bowl.

COOK'S NOTES

Cinnamon and apples add warmth and spice to whatever root vegetables you have on hand.
This dish is as simple as it is beautiful to look at.

ROASTED ROOT VEGETABLES WITH APPLES

Total Prep Time: 40 minutes
Active Time: 15 minutes
Serves: 4

Ingredients

1-2 lbs sweet potatoes or yams, scrubbed, unpeeled and cut into 2-inch chunks or wedges
1-2 lbs assorted root vegetables, peeled and cut into large chunks (about 2-inch pieces) such as carrots, parsnips, radishes, rutabaga, turnips
2 apples, scrubbed, cored and cut into 2-inch chunks
1 small bunch thyme, rinsed
1 onion, peeled and cut into large wedges
4 cloves garlic, peeled and crushed
Optional: ground cinnamon
Extra virgin olive oil (EVOO), sea salt, freshly cracked black pepper

Directions

1. Pre-heat the oven to 375 degrees
2. Peel/cut the onion, root veggies, and apples as necessary and put them in a 13 x 9 pan or other roasting dish along with a couple sprigs of thyme and the cloves of garlic. Drizzle some EVOO over them, sprinkle very generously with salt and pepper and cinnamon if using, and toss to distribute the oil and seasonings.
3. Roast approximately 30-40 minutes, until the vegetables are tender when pierced with a sharp knife. Toss the vegetables once about mid-way through cooking with a spatula to ensure even browning.

COOK'S NOTES

ROASTED ACORN SQUASH WITH MAPLE BUTTER

Total Prep Time: 25 minutes
Active Time: 15 minutes
Serves: 4

Ingredients
3 small acorn or other winter squashes
3 tablespoons butter (best from grass-fed cows)
3 tablespoons maple syrup
Cinnamon, optional
Extra virgin olive oil (EVOO), sea salt and black pepper

Directions
1. Pre-heat the oven to 425 degrees. Cut the squashes in half length-wise then scrape out the seeds and any stringy bits. Lightly oil the cut surface of the squash, sprinkle with salt and pepper, and place cut-side up on a cookie sheet or shallow baking dish. Place in the oven and bake for 35-40 minutes until a sharp knife slides easily through the squash.

2. While the squashes are cooking mash the butter and maple syrup together. When the squashes are done cooking, top with a small dollop of the maple butter and garnish with a sprinkling of cinnamon. Serve warm and enjoy.

COOK'S 🥕 NOTES

CHILI SWEET POTATO FRIES

Total Prep Time: 35 minutes
Active Time: 15 minutes
Serves: 4

Ingredients

2 large or 3 medium sweet potatoes or yams (can sub russet potatoes)

1 teaspoon chili powder

2 teaspoons garlic salt

1 teaspoon paprika

Extra virgin olive oil (EVOO), sea salt, freshly cracked black pepper

Directions

3. Pre-heat the oven to 400 degrees.

4. Scrub the potatoes, then slice them into ½ inch thick spears.

5. Place the fries on a baking sheet and drizzle with EVOO. Combine all of the seasonings with about a teaspoon of black pepper then sprinkle the seasonings over the top of the fries. Toss everything together to coat then spread into a single layer on the baking sheet.

6. Bake for 12 minutes then flip and bake for another 10-12 minutes until the fries are cooked through (pierce with a sharp knife to make sure the center is soft) and browned on the outside. Serve with ketchup and/or mustard.

COOK'S NOTES

Pesto isn't just for basil! Make a nutrient-dense pesto with kale and toss it into any grains or pasta you like. My favorite add-ins are cubed and roasted butternut squash and dried cherries.

WINTER KALE PESTO

Total Prep Time: 15 minutes
Active Time: 15 minutes
Serves: 4

Ingredients
1 bunch kale, rinsed and stems removed
½ cup toasted hulled pumpkin seeds
1/3 cup pecorino romano or parmesan cheese, grated (about 3 ounces) or sub nutritional yeast
2 cloves garlic, about 2 teaspoons minced
1 lemon, juiced
Extra virgin olive oil (EVOO), sea salt and black pepper

Directions
In a blender or food processor combine the kale, 1 tablespoon of lemon juice, pumpkin seeds, cheese, garlic, 1/3 cup EVOO, 1/4 tsp salt and some fresh black pepper. Blend until a smooth paste forms, adding more EVOO if necessary.

COOK'S NOTES

Making your own granola is easier than you'd think, and makes a fast breakfast or a filling snack. Not only does it taste better than store-bought varieties, it will have significantly less sugar and more of the good nuts and fruits that you like. I still remember my mom's homemade granola as one of my favorite breakfasts when I was younger.

HOMEMADE GRANOLA

Ingredients

6 cups rolled oats (not quick cooking or instant)

2 cups mixed nuts or seeds (almonds, walnuts, pecans, sunflower seeds, pumpkin seeds, etc)

1-2 cups dried fruit (cherries, apricots, dried cranberries, goji berries, etc) in bite-sized pieces

1 teaspoon ground cinnamon, optional

1/3 to ½ cup honey or maple syrup

½ to 2/3 cup nut butter and/or coconut oil

*If you like crunchy granola don't add any fat to the mix (oil or nut butters). If you like a chewier granola, try adding some peanut or sunflower seed butter or coconut oil.

**Have fun experimenting with different fruit and nut combinations, and try mixing it up with spices, too. Cinnamon, nutmeg, and ginger are all great options.

Directions:

1. Preheat oven to 350 degrees, if using nut butter use 325 degrees.

2. Place your sweetener, nut butter, and coconut oil if using on a small saucepan. Heat it over low heat just until everything has turned to a liquid and can easily be stirred into the oats. Add the salt and spices and stir well.

3. Place the oats in a large mixing bowl. Add the nuts and seeds if they still need to be toasted. If they're already toasted add them in later. Pour the liquid over the oats and toss well to coat.

4. Spread the mixture onto the baking sheet and bake for 10 minutes, then remove and stir the oats. Bake for an additional 5-10 minutes until the oats are toasty brown. Keep a close eye on the oats in the final minutes of cooking to prevent burning, especially if using nut butter. Add any toasted nuts and dried fruit and toss everything together.

5. Allow the granola to cool before storing in an airtight container.

COOK'S 🥕 NOTES——————————————————————————

SIMPLE HERBED QUINOA

Total Prep Time: 20 minutes
Active Time: 5 minutes
Serves: 4 or more

Ingredients (for every 1 cup quinoa):
1 3/4 cups of water or stock
½ tsp dried or 1 tablespoon fresh herbs such as rosemary or thyme
Optional: a little minced onion or garlic

Directions
Bring the water or stock to a simmer in a small saucepan with a tight-fitting lid. Add the quinoa and herbs, onions and garlic if using, and simmer covered for 15 minutes until the quinoa is cooked through. Fluff with a fork before serving.

COOK'S NOTES

My young kids weren't crazy about plain quinoa, but they scarf down these quinoa cakes. You can make them with or without the salsa, serving them with whatever condiments you like the most.

"LEFTOVER" QUINOA CAKES WITH AVOCADO-CITRUS SALSA

Total Prep Time: 30 minutes
Active Time: 25 minutes
Serves: 4

Ingredients
2-3 cups leftover cooked quinoa (from about ¾ cup dried)
2-3 eggs (1 egg per cup of quinoa)
1/2 -3/4 cups breadcrumbs or crushed puffed rice cereal
Up to 1 cup left-over or frozen thawed vegetables
2 teaspoons cumin
For the salsa:
3 oranges rind removed, segmented and cut into small pieces
½ red onion, minced
1 lime, juice and zest
1 avocado cut into small cubes
¼ cup minced cilantro or parsley
Extra virgin olive oil (EVOO), high-heat oil or butter, sea salt and black pepper

Directions
1. Combine all of the ingredients for the quinoa cakes in a large bowl along with 1 tsp of sea salt and some fresh black pepper. Mix together well and set aside to let the mixture firm up (as the breadcrumbs absorb any moisture).
2. Meanwhile place a large non-stick skillet over medium heat. Add a couple of tablespoons of a high-heat oil (canola, grapeseed) or butter, or a combination of the two. When the oil is hot, place golf-ball sized scoops of the quinoa mixture in the skillet and flatten into a cake. Let them cook for about 4 minutes per side, until lightly browned, then flip and cook the other side. Cook all of the cakes this way: you should get about 12. Add butter or oil to the pan as needed. Adjust the heat down if the quinoa cakes start to burn, and up if the cakes aren't browning fast enough. The oil should not smoke or smell funny.

COOK'S NOTES

3. While the cakes are cooking cut up and mix ingredients for the salsa. Cut the rind off of the outside of the oranges with a paring knife, then segment them by running the knife in-between the pith and the orange fruit. If you're feeling lazy, which I frequently am, you can also just cube it without segmenting. Combine the orange cubes with the juice and zest of the lime, the minced onion, the cubed avocado, and the parsley or cilantro.

4. Serve the quinoa cakes topped with the salsa and enjoy.

COOK'S NOTES

This is another versatile recipe that works as well for breakfast or brunch as it does for dinner. Leftover crepes store wonderfully in the refrigerator, so consider making extra to have on-hand for quick breakfasts during the week.

BUCKWHEAT CREPES

Total Prep Time: 25 minutes
Active Time: 25 minutes
Serves: 4

Ingredients

1 cup water
½ cup whole milk (non-dairy milk is fine too)
2 eggs
1 ¼ cups whole grain buckwheat flour, or sub whole wheat or whole spelt flour
Butter, honey, sea salt and fresh black pepper

Filling Ideas

1. Ham and Swiss: 4 ounces thinly sliced ham and 4 ounces Swiss cheese, grated
2. Smoked salmon: 4 ounces smoked salmon and 1 small container plain full-fat Greek yogurt or sour cream mixed with ¼ cup minced chives and the juice from 1 lemon
3. A few scrambled eggs
4. Nut butter and jam

Directions

1. Make the crepes: whisk together the water, milk, flour, eggs, 2 tablespoons of melted butter (melt an extra 2 tablespoons too, for cooking the crepes), 2 tsp of honey, and a pinch of salt and pepper. Beat the batter for 2-3 minutes so that it's very smooth.
2. Heat a small non-stick skillet over medium heat and brush it with melted butter. When the pan is hot, add about ¼ cup of the batter and then pick the pan up, tilting it in a circular motion so that the batter spreads around the pan in a thin layer. Cook for about 3 minutes until the crepe has lightly browned on one side and is easily flipped. The crepes will cook on the second side for only 30-60 seconds. Keep repeating until all of the crepes are cooked, lightly buttering the pan in-between each crepe (I find a silicon pastry brush is the easiest tool to use here).

COOK'S NOTES

Don't worry if the first one doesn't work out – it might take 1 or 2 to get the hang of it and to season the pan. Keep the crepes warm by stacking and covering with a kitchen towel until ready to use.

3. Fill the crepes with whatever filling you enjoy. You can fold the crepes into half-moons or quarters, or roll them.

COOK'S NOTES

My daugter, who loves mushrooms, is crazy about this dish. Mushroom stock makes an especially mushroomy risotto, but other stock will be delicious too.

BROWN RICE RISOTTO WITH WILD MUSHROOMS

Total Prep Time: 45 minutes
Active Time: 45 minutes
Serves: 4

Ingredients

1 cup uncooked brown rice, preferably short-grain

1 onion, minced

2 teaspoons minced garlic, from about 2 cloves

1 tsp dried thyme or 1 sprig fresh

8 ounces fresh mixed wild mushrooms, shitakes, or sub other mushrooms

3 cups chicken or mushroom stock

1 ½ cups frozen peas

½ cup Parmesan or pecorino romano cheese, plus extra for topping

Extra virgin olive oil (EVOO), butter, sea salt, and freshly cracked black pepper

Directions

1. Bring a medium pot of at least 6 cups of water to a boil and add the brown rice. Simmer for 20 minutes and then drain the rice (at this point it's partially cooked).

2. While the rice is cooking, sauté the mushrooms and onions in a little EVOO and/or butter (about 2-3 tablespoons total), in the same pan until the mushrooms are browned and the onions have softened. Season the mushrooms and onions with some salt, pepper, and the thyme while they're cooking. Add the garlic for the last 2 minutes of sautéing. The whole process will probably take about 8-10 minutes.

3. Place the stock in a small saucepan over low heat. Heat the stock until it's warm but not yet simmering.

4. When the mushrooms are lightly browned and tasty (taste one!) and the rice is done, add the rice to the sauté pan and sauté it over medium heat for a few minutes until it's coated with a little of the oil from the pan. You can add a little more if the pan is totally dry. Then slowly begin adding the stock, in ½ -3/4 cup increments. Stir the rice until the stock is absorbed, about 3 minutes per addition. Keep adding the stock and slowly stirring until it has all been absorbed (think of this as a relaxing, meditative experience!). The rice will release some starch and

COOK'S NOTES

the mixture should be loose but not too soupy. Taste the rice to ensure that it's al dente, but cooked all the way. If you run out of stock before the rice is done to your liking, you can add warmed water until the rice is finished.

5. Add the peas and ½ cup of the parmesan and stir until the peas are warmed through. Then taste, adjust salt, pepper and parmesan to taste and serve.

COOK'S NOTES

FARRO SALAD WITH SHERRY VINAIGRETTE

Total Prep Time: 45 minutes
Active Time: 15 minutes
Serves: 4

Ingredients

*1 ½ cups semi-pearled farro (for GF, sub brown rice or quinoa)
1 bunch asparagus spears, tough ends removed (approx. bottom 1-2 inches) and cut into 2-inch pieces
1 pint cherry tomatoes, halved
6 ounces fresh feta cheese, crumbled, optional
4 cups baby spinach leaves, rinsed and patted or spun dry
¼ cup sherry vinegar
1 tablespoon honey
½ red onion, thinly sliced
1 tsp minced or grated garlic from about 1 clove
Extra virgin olive oil (EVOO), sea salt, freshly cracked black pepper

Directions

1. In a medium saucepan with a lid, place 3 cups of water and ½ tsp salt and bring to a boil. Add the farro, reduce to a simmer, cover and cook for 35-40 minutes until the grains are tender. Check the grains once 2/3 way through cooking to ensure that the grains don't need any more water. When they're fully cooked, strain any excess liquid and let the steam evaporate.

2. Meanwhile, whisk together the vinegar, ½ cup of EVOO, honey, garlic, and pinches of salt and pepper. Set aside.

3. Steam the asparagus: this can be done either in a separate pan, using ½ inch of water on the bottom of the pan, or in the same pan as the grains. If using a separate pan, bring the ½ inch of water to a simmer, add the asparagus and a tight lid, and steam for about 3 minutes until the asparagus is bright green and crisp tender. If using the same pan as the grains, add the asparagus to the top of the grains for the final 5 minutes of cooking.

4. Place the cooked grains, asparagus, spinach, cherry tomatoes, and sliced onions in a large bowl. Add the dressing and toss to combine. Gently fold or toss in the feta.

5. Can be served immediately or chilled and served up to 24 hours later.

COOK'S NOTES

QUINOA WALDORF SALAD WITH APPLES, WALNUTS AND SPINACH

Total Prep Time: 40 minutes
Active Time: 30 minutes
Serves: 4 with leftovers

Ingredients
1 1/2 cups uncooked quinoa
1 cup chopped walnuts
1 medium apple, cored and chopped small
½ cup raisins or dried cranberries
4 cups packed baby spinach leaves, about 4 ounces, roughly chopped
½ cup minced fresh parsley
3 tablespoons apple cider vinegar
1/3 cup apple juice or apple cider
Juice of ½ lemon
1/2 tsp cinnamon
¼ tsp nutmeg
Extra virgin olive oil (EVOO), sea salt, freshly cracked black pepper

Directions
1. Place the quinoa in a fine-mesh sieve and rinse it in cool water until the water runs clear. Place 2 ½ cups of water and 1 teaspoon of salt in a medium saucepan and bring to a simmer. Add the quinoa, return to a simmer, cover and cook for 15 minutes. Pour the quinoa back into the fine-mesh sieve to let the steam evaporate and the quinoa cool slightly.

2. While the quinoa is cooking chop the other ingredients.

3. Whisk together the apple cider vinegar, apple juice or cider, lemon juice, cinnamon, nutmeg, ¼ cup EVOO, ½ tsp salt and some fresh black pepper.

4. Place the spinach leaves, walnuts, raisins or cranberries, and parsley in a large bowl. Top with the cooked quinoa and add the dressing. Toss everything to combine. The flavors of the salad will meld, and the dressing continues to absorb, the longer the salad sits, so this is a good recipe to prepare a few hours or even a day in advance.

COOK'S NOTES

BARLEY SALAD WITH ZUCCHINI, TOMATO, MOZZARELLA AND BASIL

Total Prep Time: 45 minutes
Active Time: 15 minutes
Serves: 4

Ingredients

1 cup semi-pearled barley or sub uncooked quinoa

1 medium zucchini, sliced in half length-wise then into ¼ inch thick rounds

1 ½ cups cherry tomatoes halved, or 1 large heirloom tomato cut into bite-sized pieces

6-8 ounces fresh mozzarella pearls, optional

1 cup basil leaves (1/2 cup for dressing and ½ cup sliced into thin strips or torn into small pieces)

¼ cup white wine vinegar

1 tablespoon honey

5 cups spinach or salad greens

Extra virgin olive oil (EVOO), sea salt, freshly cracked black pepper

Directions

1. Cook your grains per package instructions (typically boil either grain in 2+ cups water for 15-20 minutes until tender). Drain the grains into a fine-mesh sieve when cooked and let steam evaporate for a few minutes.

2. Optional: broil vegetables (if you like cooked or sweeter vegetables this is a good step to take. If you prefer raw, simply skip this step.) Pre-heat your oven to 400 degrees. Toss the vegetables in a little EVOO, salt and pepper until well-coated then spread single-layer on a baking sheet. Roast for 15 minutes until the vegetables are tender.

3. Make a basil vinaigrette: combine ½ cup whole basil leaves with the white wine vinegar, honey, and ½ cup EVOO. Blend in a food processor or blender until well-com-bined. Season with some salt and pepper.

4. Toss the warm grains with the vegetables, vinaigrette, and remaining sliced basil. Serve at room temperature overtop a small pile of spinach or salad greens.

COOK'S NOTES

I love a frittata. They're so much easier than quiche but have the same versatility. Throw one together in just a few minutes for brunch, lunch or dinner and you'll have something a little extra special without the extra work.

WILD MUSHROOM AND SWISS FRITTATA

Total Prep Time: 30 minutes
Active Time: 15 minutes
Serves: 4

Ingredients

1 lb fresh wild mushrooms, such as oyster (can sub baby bella), thinly sliced or torn into bite-sized pieces

8 eggs, preferably from pasture raised and cage-free hens

4 ounces Swiss cheese, grated

1 tsp dried thyme

1 teaspoon grated or minced garlic, from about 1 clove

1 small onion or ½ large onion, about 1 cup thinly sliced

1 cup milk

Hot sauce, optional

Extra virgin olive oil (EVOO), sea salt, freshly cracked black pepper

Directions

1. Pre-heat the oven to 400 degrees.

2. To bake the frittata it's easiest to use an oven-proof 10-inch skillet. If you don't have one that's oven-proof (it can not have any plastic pieces such as handles), you can use a pie pan. If using a pie pan grease it lightly with a little EVOO.

3. Place a sauté pan over medium heat and add a little EVOO. Add the mushrooms, thyme, and a pinch of salt and pepper and sauté, stirring regularly, until the mushrooms have released their moisture, about 8 minutes. Move the mushrooms to a bowl and add the onions to the pan along with a little more EVOO.

4. Sauté the onions until they're translucent and softened, about 4 minutes. Add the mushrooms back to the pan and toss them together with the onions so they're evenly combined. Turn off the heat temporarily. **If baking in a pie pan**, transfer everything now and proceed with the following steps in the pie pan.

COOK'S NOTES

5. Top the onions and mushrooms with the grated swiss cheese. Beat the eggs together with the milk, ½ tsp salt, several grinds of fresh black pepper, and a few dashes of hot sauce until everything is well combined. Pour the eggs over top of the mushrooms, onions and cheese. Turn the stove back on med-low and cook until the bottom of the frittata firms up, about 3 minutes (you'll see it just begin to cook along the sides). Transfer to the oven and bake for 15-17 minutes until the top of the frittata has firmed up and is puffed in the center. If using a pie pan the frittata will have to bake in its entirety in the oven, so will take an additional 5-10 minutes.

6. Let sit for 3-5 minutes before slicing and serving.

*Use any combination of veggies, cheese and herbs you like. I also love broccoli and cheddar, asparagus and goat cheese, and spinach with anything

COOK'S NOTES

Baked eggs make a convenient and delicious meal at any time of day. I'll even prepare them for a nice brunch with guests, and everyone enjoys having their own special dish.

BAKED EGGS WITH SPINACH AND NUTMEG

Total Prep Time: 35 minutes
Active Time: 20 minutes
Serves: 4

Ingredients

1 lb fresh spinach
4-8 eggs, depending on how many each person would like
3-4 tablespoons heavy cream
1 small or ½ medium onion, about 1 cup minced
1 teaspoon minced garlic
¼ tsp ground fresh nutmeg
Extra virgin olive oil (EVOO), sea salt, freshly cracked black pepper

Directions

1. Lightly oil or butter 4 8-ounce ramekins and pre-heat your oven to 400 degrees. If you don't have ramekins, you can also use ceramic oven-proof mugs or muffin tins.

2. Place a large sauté pan over medium-low heat. Add the minced onion and sauté until very tender, about 4 minutes. Add the garlic and sauté for one more minute then add the spinach. Season the spinach with the nutmeg and some salt and pepper and sauté until most of the moisture from the spinach has been released and evaporated, about 7 minutes. Taste the spinach and adjust salt and pepper to taste.

3. Divide the spinach equally among the ramekins.

4. Carefully crack one egg at a time into a small bowl, taking care not to break the yolk. Make a small well in the spinach in each ramekin and carefully slide one egg from the bowl into each of the wells.

5. Top the eggs with equal amounts of cream, about 2 teaspoons per ramekin.

6. Bake the eggs in the center of the oven until the whites are completely set, about 15 minutes. The yolks will be slightly runny. Serve right away, but be careful when handling hot ramekins!

COOK'S NOTES

Sardines are a pantry staple in my house. They're a true superfood, high in omega-3s and calcium, and because they're so small, low in contaminants like mercury. I make this tuna-salad like spread and eat it on open faced sandwiches with rye bread and a little melted Swiss cheese.

SARDINE SPREAD WITH LEMON AND PARSLEY

Total Prep Time: 10 minutes
Active Time: 10 minutes
Serves: 4

Ingredients

2 small cans of Sardines, packed in oil
2 teaspoons mustard
2 teaspoons fresh lemon juice
3 tablespoons minced onion, chives, or green onions
1 tablespoon minced fresh parsley
Sea salt and black pepper

Directions

Mash the sardines with a fork and combine with other ingredients. Season with sea salt and fresh black pepper. Spread onto a dense whole-grain bread or toast, then serve warm.

COOK'S NOTES

During the fall and winter I roast a chicken once or twice a month. It makes the house smell great, everyone loves it, and it provides the raw ingredients for home-made chicken stock that makes the base of my soups and stews.

SIMPLE ROASTED CHICKEN

Total Prep Time: 1 hour 5 minutes
Active Time: 15 minutes
Serves: 4

Ingredients
1 5-6 lb roasting chicken, pasture-raised and hormone and antibiotic free is best
1 lemon, sliced in half
1 small onion, quartered
1 head garlic, cut in half cross-wise
Optional: dried or fresh herbs (thyme, rosemary, oregano, etc)
Extra virgin olive oil (EVOO), sea salt and black pepper

Directions
1. Preheat your oven to 400 degrees
2. Pat the chicken dry, and liberally salt and pepper the inside cavity (make sure giblets are removed). Stuff the chicken cavity with the lemon slices, quartered onion, and garlic.
3. Rub EVOO over the outside of the chicken and sprinkle with salt and pepper.
4. Place the chicken on a roasting rack set inside a roasting pan. You can also rest the chicken atop a bed of chopped onions, potatoes, or root vegetables and let them roast together. If using a meat thermometer (highly recommended), place the probe deep in the thigh of the chicken as close to the bone as possible. Place the chicken on the rack and place in the oven.
5. Roast for approximately 50-60 minutes (slightly less if the chicken is smaller, and more if the chicken is larger), until the juices run clear when you cut between the thigh and leg, or until your meat thermometer reads 165 degrees; make sure the thermometer is deep in the thigh – if the temperature is rising suspiciously fast and 165 is reached very quickly, the thermometer might be too shallow.
6. It's best to let the chicken rest for 10 minutes, so that the juices can redistribute and settle, before carving.

COOK'S NOTES

It's a great idea to make a big pot of this and save a few servings in the freezer. You'll have an easy and nourishing meal when a cold or flu arises.

IMMUNITY-BOOSTING CHICKEN SOUP

Total Prep Time: 1 day, 35 minutes including stock preparation
Active Time: 35 minutes
Serves: 4

Ingredients

Leftover chicken carcass and bones from 1 roasted chicken, or 1 lb chicken bones

2-3 cups left-over chicken meat cut into bite-sized pieces

1 lb shitake mushrooms, stems removed and reserved

2 carrots, thinly sliced

1 onion, chopped

2 stalks celery, thinly sliced

4 teaspoons minced garlic, from about 4 cloves

1 2-inch piece fresh ginger, grated

1 lb russet or new potatoes, scrubbed and cut into ¾ inch cubes

1 bay leaf

Optional: 1 piece kombu (seaweed)

Extra virgin olive oil (EVOO), sea salt and black pepper

Directions

1. **1- 3 days before eating the soup**: Place the chicken bones or carcass in a large stock pot along with the shitake mushroom stems. Add a tablespoon of vinegar then bring to a boil. Cover, reduce to a simmer, and cook for 8-24 hours. Add more water as needed to keep the bones covered with water. You'll want 2-3 quarts of stock by the time you're done.

2. When the stock is finished strain the liquid into a large bowl and discard the solids. Stock will keep covered in the fridge for up to 3 days. Any fat in the stock will rise to the top and turn solid once cold, at which point you can skim it off the top, however if you use bones without skin, there will only be trace amounts of fat and this probably won't be necessary. You can also place the stock in glass canning jars and freeze for use later.

3. **Day-of:** Thinly slice the heads of the shitake mushrooms. Heat a large soup pot over medium heat and add a drizzle of EVOO. Add the mushrooms and sauté for

COOK'S NOTES

5-8 minutes until they soften. Add the onions, carrots, celery, garlic and ginger and continue to sauté until the vegetables become tender, an additional 5 minutes. Add the potatoes, kombu, bay leaf, a tablespoon of salt, some fresh black pepper, and 2 quarts of chicken stock and bring to a simmer. Simmer until the potatoes are tender, about 15 minutes. Add the chicken meat and bring back to a simmer for another minute.

4. Remove the kombu before serving. Add additional salt and pepper to taste. This soup is also tasty served with a little hot sauce, some grated parmesan cheese, and/ or a tablespoon of tomato salsa.

COOK'S NOTES

SALMON AND BLACK BEAN BURGERS

Total Prep Time: 25 minutes
Active Time: 15 minutes
Serves: 4

Ingredients

16 ounces canned wild Alaskan salmon, picked clean of stray skin*

1 ½ cups cooked black beans, from 1 can or ½ cup dried

1/3 cup minced onion, about ½ of 1 small

1 ¼ teaspoons ground cumin

3 limes, juice and zest

1/3 cup instant oats, or 1 cup breadcrumbs

1 egg lightly beaten

¼ cup minced fresh cilantro

½ tsp minced garlic, from 1 small clove

5 ounces arugula

2 large heirloom tomatoes or 1 cup cherry tomatoes

High heat oil (canola or grapeseed), sea salt and black pepper

Directions

1. Place the canned salmon in a medium mixing bowl. Using a fork, break up the salmon and mash any large bones into the mixture.

2. Mash ½ of the black beans with the back of a fork then add them to the salmon along with the remaining beans, minced onion, 1 tsp cumin, juice and zest of 1 lime, oats or breadcrumbs, egg, cilantro, about ½ tsp salt, and some black pepper. Mix everything together well and set aside for a couple of minutes

3. Whisk together ¼ cup EVOO, juice from the remaining 2 limes, the minced garlic, pinches of salt and pepper, and the remaining ¼ tsp cumin.

4. Place a large skillet over medium heat and add a few tablespoons of high-heat oil. Pack the salmon and black bean burgers into a 1/3 cup measure and drop them onto the skillet. Flatten them out to about ¾ inch thick and cook until lightly browned, about 3-4 minutes, then flip and cook on the other side. If the burgers aren't holding together well you can always add a little more oats or breadcrumbs, if too wet, or another egg, if dry. They may be a little fragile until they begin to

COOK'S NOTES—

cook through, so be sure to cook them well on the first side so that they begin to set up.

5. Serve the salmon burgers over a bed of arugula and tomato and drizzled with the dressing.

*Don't worry about bones – just mash them into the mixture – they're very soft and add great calcium to the dish

COOK'S NOTES

APPLE MUSTARD BRINED PORK TENDERLOIN

Total Prep Time: 1 day 20 minutes
Active Time: 20 minutes
Serves: 4

Ingredients

2 cups apple cider or apple juice, preferably organic

1-1 ½ lbs pork tenderloin (or sub 1 lb seitan or extra-firm tofu)

¼ cup sea salt

¼ cup maple syrup, or sub brown sugar or honey

2 teaspoons black pepper

1 teaspoon crushed red pepper

2 tablespoons mustard

Extra virgin olive oil (EVOO), sea salt, freshly cracked black pepper

Directions

Day Before: Place the apple cider, salt, sugar, peppers, and mustard in a sauce pan and bring to a simmer. Stir the mixture until the salt and sugar are dissolved. Remove from the stove then add 1 cup of water and 2 cups of ice and wait for the ice to dissolve and the mixture to cool down. Place the pork and marinade in a snug airtight container with a lid to marinate overnight. If using meat substitute, cut the salt by ½, don't add the extra water and ice, but do let the mixture cool slightly.

Day of Eating:

1. Pre-heat your oven to 425 degrees or heat your grill, and remove the pork from the marinade. Roast in the oven in a roasting dish until the pork reaches 145 degrees in the very center, about 15-20 minutes, or grill on a greased grill until 145 degrees in the center. The pork will continue to cook and go up approximately 5 degrees.

2. If grilling tofu, press the marinated tofu between dry paper towels for several minutes before grilling (one easy method is to set a plate with a can of beans on top). Grill both tofu and seitan until heated through and crispy on the outside.

3. Let the pork rest for about 5 minutes before slicing into ½ inch slices. Delicious served over rice.

COOK'S NOTES

This recipe is so easy, quick and tasty that sometimes I have to remind myself to make salmon in different ways. The honey mustard adds just the right amount of sweetness, and you can serve extra on the side for dipping.

BAKED HONEY MUSTARD SALMON

Total Prep Time: 20 minutes
Active Time: 10 minutes
Serves: 4

Ingredients
1 ¼ lbs wild salmon filets
2 tablespoons yellow or Dijon mustard
1 ½ tablespoons honey, raw and local is best
Extra virgin olive oil (EVOO), sea salt, freshly cracked black pepper

Directions
1. Pre-heat your oven to 375 degrees
2. Pat the salmon filets dry, then place skin-side down in a shallow baking dish that has been greased with a little oil, such as a 13 x 9 inch pan.
3. Whisk together the mustard, honey, horseradish if using, and 1 tsp salt. Add a little black pepper, or if you like spice 1/4 – ½ tsp crushed red pepper. Spread it evenly over the flesh of the salmon with the back of a spoon.
4. Bake until the salmon is cooked through, about 10 minutes for individual filets or up to 20 for one large filet. Check the salmon in the middle with a fork or sharp knife for doneness. If the flesh is still a bright reddish-orange it will need to cook a little longer.

COOK'S NOTES

BISON MEAT LOAF WITH GARLIC AND WORCESTERSHIRE

Total Prep Time: 55 minutes
Active Time: 25 minutes
Serves: 4

Ingredients

1 - 1½ lbs ground bison meat

8 ounces pre-sliced mushrooms, chopped

¾ cup shredded carrot, from about 2 full carrots

1 small onion, diced

2 slices stale whole wheat bread, torn into breadcrumbs (or sub 1 cup brown rice crisp cereal for *GF)

½ cup milk

1 egg

3 teaspoons minced garlic, from about 3 cloves

3 tablespoons Worcestershire

1 large tomato, sliced

Ketchup

Extra virgin olive oil (EVOO), sea salt and black pepper

Directions

1. Pre-heat the oven to 375 degrees.

2. Put the fresh breadcrumbs in a bowl and drizzle with the milk. Set aside to soak.

3. Heat some EVOO in a large saucepan over medium heat. Sauté the onions, mushrooms and carrots for about 5 minutes until they begin to soften. Add the garlic and sauté another minute. Season with a little sea salt and black pepper then set aside to cool.

4. In a large mixing bowl, break up the bison lightly with a fork. Gently squeeze the bread crumbs to release extra milk, and add them to the bowl. Add the sautéed vegetables and the egg, along with 1 1/2 teaspoons of salt, the Worcestershire and lots of fresh black pepper. Mix everything gently together until combined. Place in a greased loaf pan and smooth the top. Drizzle a little ketchup on top of the loaf and then layer with sliced tomatoes. Bake until the inside registers 160 degrees, about 50 minutes.

COOK'S NOTES

LIME AND CUMIN MARINATED FLANK STEAK

Total Prep Time: 25 minutes plus overnight marinating
Active Time: 25 minutes
Serves: 4

Ingredients

1 – 1 ½ lb flank steak, from grass-fed beef or bison (can also substitute seitan)

1 tsp ground cumin

2 tsp minced garlic, from about 2 cloves

1 tablespoon Worcestershire

¼ cup lime juice from about 3 limes

Extra virgin olive oil (EVOO), sea salt, freshly cracked black pepper

Directions

1. **Night before**: whisk together the lime juice, 1/3 cup EVOO, cumin, garlic, Worcestershire, 2 tsp of salt and lots of fresh black pepper. Place the steak in a glass or ceramic baking dish – preferably one with a tight-fitting lid – and pour the marinade over the steak. For best marinating choose a dish that will allow the steak to fit snugly with the marinade. Cover and let the steak marinate overnight. If you remember to, you can flip the steak in the morning to ensure that the other side is fully marinated.

2. When you're ready to cook: pre-heat your broiler or grill. If broiling, broil the steak 5-6 inches from the top of the oven about 7 minutes on each side until medium (135 degrees) – note that cooking times will depend on the thickness of the steak. If grilling, grill approximately 5 minutes per side for medium (again noting that steak thickness and exact grill heat will determine exact cooking time).

3. Let the steak rest for approximately 5 minutes before slicing, to allow for juices to settle.

COOK'S 🥕 NOTES

Another favorite go-to meal that's great when you're under time pressure, this soup can be made in less than 10 minutes of prep time if you have the ingredients in the pantry.

QUICK BLACK BEAN SOUP WITH TOMATOES AND CUMIN

Total Prep Time: 30 minutes
Active Time: 10 minutes
Serves: 4

Ingredients

1 medium onion, chopped
3 cloves garlic, minced, or 1 tablespoon jarred minced garlic
2 sprigs fresh thyme, or 2 teaspoons dried
4 ½ cups cooked black beans, from 3 cans or 1 ½ cups dried
1 quart water or broth/stock (chicken or vegetable)
28 ounces canned chopped or crushed tomatoes
1 tablespoon ground cumin
Hot sauce and plain yogurt or sour cream, optional
Extra virgin olive oil (EVOO), sea salt, freshly cracked black pepper

Directions

1. Place a medium-large soup pot over medium heat on the stove. Add a large drizzle of EVOO and sauté the onion until it softens, about 4 minutes. Add the garlic and thyme and sauté for another minute until fragrant. Add the tomatoes, beans, stock, cumin, two teaspoons of salt and some black pepper, and bring to a simmer. If you like a spicy soup, add several shakes of hot sauce.

2. Simmer the soup uncovered for at least 15 minutes until the flavors are well-combined and the beans and tomatoes begin to break down. Puree the soup with an immersion blender and taste it, adjusting salt, pepper and hot sauce to taste.

3. Serve topped with a tablespoon of sour cream, optional.

4. This soup is delicious served with grilled cheese for dipping.

COOK'S NOTES

SPIT PEA SOUP WITH THYME AND CARROTS

Total Prep Time: 2 hours
Active Time: 15 minutes
Serves: 4

Ingredients

1 small onion, minced

1 tsp minced garlic, from about 1 clove

2 bay leaves

2 sprigs fresh thyme, or 2 teaspoons dried

3 carrots, sliced into half moons

1 2-lb ham hock, or ¾ ham steak cubed, optional

2 cups green or yellow split peas

2 quarts water

Extra virgin olive oil (EVOO), sea salt, freshly cracked black pepper and crushed red pepper

Directions

1. In a large soup pot, heat 2 tablespoons of EVOO over medium heat. Sauté the onion and carrots for 4-5 minutes, until they begin to soften. Add the other ingredients along with 1 tablespoon of sea salt, several grinds of black pepper, and a pinch of crushed red pepper and bring to a boil.

2. Reduce to a simmer and cover. Simmer, stirring occasionally, until the yellow peas dissolve and form a thick soup, about 1 ½ hours.

3. Remove the ham hock and, when it's cool enough to handle, cut the meat off the bone into bite-sized pieces. Add them back into the soup.

4. Serve warm with a crusty whole grain bread.

5. **Slow cooker alternative**: combine all ingredients in a slow cooker and cook on high for 6 hours. Remove ham hock and shred meat before serving.

COOK'S 🥕 NOTES

Homemade hummus is fun to customize with flavors you like, super cheap, and even stores well in the freezer. Use it as a dip or a spread on sandwiches or wraps.

HOMEMADE HUMMUS

Total Prep Time: 15 minutes
Active Time: 15 minutes
Serves: 4

Ingredients

3 cups cooked chickpeas, from about 2 cans or 1 cup dried, *about ½ cup of cooking liquid reserved
2 cloves garlic
Juice from 1-2 lemons, about ¼ cup or more to taste
¼ cup tahini (sesame seed paste, look by the nut butters in the grocery store)
1 teaspoon salt
Optional: 1 tsp ground cumin or other spices/herbs you enjoy
Extra virgin olive oil (EVOO), sea salt, freshly cracked black pepper, hot sauce, optional

Directions

Place the chickpeas, garlic, salt, ¼ cup of lemon juice, tahini, ¼ cup of EVOO, and about ¼ cup of reserved liquid in a blender or food processor. Process until smooth, adding more cooking liquid and/or EVOO and/or lemon juice to taste. Season as needed with black pepper or hot sauce.

COOK'S NOTES

Roasted garbanzo beans make a delicious and even addictive snack. They're best the day you make them when they're still warm, and you won't have any problem eating them all.

ROASTED GARBANZO BEANS

Total Prep Time: 20-25 minutes
Active Time: 5 minutes
Serves: 4

Ingredients
1 12 ounce can garbanzo beans, drained
1 tablespoons olive oil
1 tsp cumin
Garlic salt
Crushed red pepper flakes, optional
¼ cup pistachios
Extra virgin olive oil (EVOO), sea salt and black pepper

Directions
1. Preheat oven or toaster oven to 400 degrees F
2. Rinse chickpeas and drain well, roll on a clean towel to dry
3. Put chickpeas in a bowl, toss with olive oil, and season to taste with seasonings.
4. Spread on a baking sheet, and bake for 20 to 25 minutes, until browned and crunchy. Check the chickpeas occasionally and shake the pan to rotate. Add pistachios for the last 5-10 minutes.

A few ideas:
1) Experiment with different seasonings, and change the quantities to suit your tastes.
2) Try curry powder, paprika, Cajun seasonings, and anything else that you enjoy!
3) Depending on your oven temp and the humidity, the time in the oven could vary by 5-15 minutes. Just taste the beans every so often and take them out when they're done to your liking.

COOK'S NOTES

The flavor combinations in this soup are just wonderful. The soup is warming and substantial but will leave you feeling light and nourished.

RED LENTIL AND COCONUT CREAM SOUP

Adapted from Coconut Red-Lentil Curry, Gourmet 2006
Total Prep Time: 30 minutes
Active Time: 20 minutes
Serves: 4 with leftovers

Ingredients

1 onion, cut into small dice

2-inch piece fresh ginger, grated fine

2 teaspoons minced garlic

1 teaspoon ground cumin

¾ teaspoon ground coriander seed

1 teaspoon turmeric

1 jalapeno, minced (can omit or remove seeds if you prefer less spice)

1 ½ cups dried red lentils

1 13 ounce can full-fat coconut milk

1 ½ cups cooked garbanzo beans, from 1 can or ½ cup dried (rinse and strain the beans if canned)

8 ounces fresh spinach, chopped into bite-sized pieces

Extra virgin olive oil (EVOO), sea salt, freshly cracked black pepper

Directions

1. Place a medium-large soup pan over medium heat and add a large drizzle of EVOO. Add the chopped onions and the garbanzo beans and sauté until the onions are softened and fragrant and the garbanzo beans are lightly golden.

2. Add the ginger, garlic, jalapeno, cumin, coriander and turmeric and sauté until the spices become fragrant, but don't let the garlic become burned, another 2-3 minutes.

3. Add the coconut milk, 2 cups of water, lentils, and a teaspoon of salt along with some fresh black pepper, and bring to a simmer. Allow the lentils to simmer, covered, for about 15 minutes until they are completely tender and begin to break apart.

4. Stir in the spinach and season with salt and pepper to taste. Allow the soup to simmer for another 3-5 minutes, just until the spinach is tender. Serve warm or at room temperature.

COOK'S 🥕 NOTES—————————————————————————————

TOMATO CHICKPEAS WITH SPINACH

Total Prep Time: 20 minutes
Active Time: 20 minutes
Serves: 4

Ingredients

1 medium onion, diced small

1 3-inch piece freshly grated ginger

3 cloves chopped or grated garlic (or canned minced)

¼ - ½ c water

1/3 cup tomato paste

1 lb fresh spinach greens, chopped

3 teaspoons chili powder

3 cups cooked chickpeas, from 2 cans or 1 cup dried

Extra virgin olive oil (EVOO), sea salt, freshly cracked black pepper

Directions

1. In a large skillet sauté the onion in a couple tablespoons of olive oil until softened. Add garlic, ginger, pinch of crushed red pepper and chili powder and sauté an additional minute until fragrant.

2. Add the tomato paste, chickpeas and spinach. Cook until the spinach wilts. Add a little water if the mixture starts to look dry (the spinach will also release some water as it wilts). Cook until everything is warmed through, and most of the liquid is evaporated (about 5 minutes). Season with salt and black pepper. Delicious served with brown rice.

COOK'S NOTES

MUJADARA LENTILS WITH CARAMELIZED ONIONS

Total Prep Time: 35 minutes
Active Time: 30 minutes
Serves: 4

Ingredients

1 medium onion, chopped into small dice

3 cloves garlic, minced

1 tablespoon cumin

1 teaspoon cinnamon

½ teaspoon allspice

1 cup dried lentils

1 bay leaf

3 medium-large onions, thinly sliced

3 cups chicken stock, vegetable stock or water

Extra virgin olive oil (EVOO) sea salt and black pepper

Directions

1. In a large skillet or pot with a lid, sauté the diced onions with a tablespoon of olive oil. When they're soft (2-3 min), add the garlic, spices, bay leaf, some salt and pepper, and the lentils. Add the water or stock, bring to a simmer, and cover to cook for 20 minutes until the lentils are cooked through.

2. Caramelize the sliced onions: use the largest skillet you have, heat ¼ cup of EVOO over medium heat, add onions and let them cook, stirring occasionally. Cook until they're caramelized and sweet, stirring regularly and adjusting the heat down if the onions start to burn and up if they're not progressing. This will take about 20 minutes.

3. Serve the lentils topped with the caramelized onions and serve with brown rice or another grain you enjoy.

COOK'S NOTES

Black-eyed peas are so simple but have such wonderful flavor. In this dish they pair nicely with the robust flavors of kielbasa, although you can certainly omit this sausage for a vegetarian version. For added convenience look for fully cooked but frozen black-eyed peas, which will thaw in minutes in the sauté pan.

HOPPIN JOHN: BLACK EYED PEAS WITH SAUSAGE

Total Prep Time: 35 minutes
Active Time: 20 minutes
Serves: 4

Ingredients
1 cup dried black eyed peas soaked overnight, or 3 cups cooked (frozen are recommended)
1 small onion, minced
2 stalks celery, sliced thinly
2 teaspoons minced garlic, from about 2 cloves
2 bay leaves
1 jalapeno, minced, optional (don't use the seeds if you like the flavor but don't want it too spicy)
4 cups chicken or vegetable stock
6 ounces kielbasa, can sub vegetarian sausage if you like, cut into ¼ inch rounds
1 cup white basmati rice, rinsed well
Hot sauce, optional
Extra virgin olive oil (EVOO), sea salt, freshly cracked black pepper

Directions
1. Place a large sauté pan – one that has a lid – over medium-low heat and add a little EVOO. Sauté the onion and celery until tender and fragrant, about 3 minutes. Add the garlic and sauté another minute. Add the sausage, bay leaves, jalapeno, and black eyed peas.

    a. **IF** using cooked back eyed peas (from frozen or canned) add the rice and 2 ½ cups of stock and bring to a simmer. Cover and cook until the rice is cooked through, about 18 minutes. Check after about 12 minutes and add liquid if the rice is dry.

COOK'S NOTES

b. **IF** using dried and soaked black eyed peas add the full 4 cups of stock and bring to a simmer. Cover and cook until the black eyed peas are almost cooked through, but not quite. Then add the rice and another ½ cup of water and continue to simmer, covered, until the both the rice and the peas are tender. Also check the Hoppin John about 10 minutes after adding the rice to add more water, if necessary.

2. Season the Hoppin John with salt, pepper and hot sauce to taste before serving.

COOK'S NOTES

POLENTA PIZZA WITH MUSHROOMS, OLIVES AND RED ONION

Total Prep Time: 50 minutes
Active Time: 30 minutes
Serves: 4

Ingredients

1 cup coarse corn meal (aka polenta)

1 tsp garlic, minced

½ cup whole milk, optional (can sub water)

2 ½ cups chicken stock or water

16 ounces fresh sliced mushrooms (baby bella, shiitake, oyster, etc)

½ cup black olives, pitted

1 small red onion, sliced

6 ounces fresh mozzarella cheese, or 4 ounces aged/shredded

1 cup homemade or other tomato sauce

Extra virgin olive oil (EVOO), sea salt, freshly cracked black pepper

Directions

1. Pre-heat your oven to 375 degrees and either grease a large baking sheet with a little EVOO or cover with a piece of parchment paper.

2. Place 2 ½ cups of stock or water in a medium saucepan, add the milk (or sub water), 3/4 tsp of salt, 1 tsp minced garlic, and bring to a simmer. While whisking constantly add the corn meal in a slow stream. Whisk until all lumps are gone and the cornmeal begins to thicken. Cook the cornmeal on a low simmer for 5 minutes and then remove from the heat. Spread the polenta with a spatula (you might have to grease the spatula with a little oil) into a pizza crust shape on the cookie sheet/parchment paper. The crust should be about ½ inch thick. It doesn't have to be perfect. Bake the crust for 25 minutes.

3. While the crust is baking place a large sauté pan over medium-low heat. Sauté the mushrooms in a little EVOO until they release their moisture and have lightly caramelized, about 8 minutes. Season them with a little salt and pepper while they're cooking and stir regularly.

COOK'S NOTES

4. Remove the crust from the oven when it's done and drizzle it with a little EVOO – brush the oil across the top of the crust if you have a pastry brush. Top with the tomato sauce, mushrooms, sliced onions, olives and cheese.

5. Bake the pizza for about 15-20 minutes until the cheese has melted and the crust is firm.

6. To prevent the crust from getting soggy on the bottom you can slide the pizza onto a cooling rack.

COOK'S NOTES

This is one of my top go-to meals if I'm in a time crunch. Pop open a can of coconut milk, add a spoonful of curry and whatever frozen or chopped vegetables I have on hand along with some lentils, and dinner is ready in less than 30 minutes.

LENTIL AND POTATO CURRY WITH COCONUT MILK

Total Prep Time: 25 minutes
Active Time: 20 minutes
Serves: 4

Ingredients
1 cup dried lentils, rinsed
1 can coconut milk – not light
2 cups chicken/vegetable broth or water
1 tablespoon curry powder
2 teaspoons garlic, from about 2 cloves
1 medium onion, diced
2 medium russet potatoes, scrubbed and diced
1 lb frozen broccoli florets, thawed, or sub fresh
¼ tsp crushed red pepper, optional
Extra virgin olive oil (EVOO), sea salt and black pepper

Directions
1. In a large sauté pan with a lid, heat a large drizzle of EVOO and sauté the onion until softened, about 4 minutes. Add the garlic and sauté another minute.

2. Add the coconut milk, broth or water, curry powder, lentils, potatoes, and crushed red pepper and bring to a simmer. Cover and simmer for 20 minutes.

4. Taste lentils and potatoes: if they're done or very close, add salt and pepper to taste, along with the broccoli (otherwise continue to cook 5 more minutes then proceed). Cover and simmer another 3-4 minutes with the broccoli until heated through.

COOK'S NOTES

CURRIED CHICKEN, POTATO AND GREEN BEAN SALAD

Total Prep Time: 25 minutes
Active Time: 15 minutes
Serves: 4

Ingredients

1 1/2 cups leftover shredded chicken (or 1 c meat substitute)
1 lb potatoes (small red or yellow new potatoes are best), scrubbed
½ lb green beans, trimmed and cut in half
1/4 cup mayo (canola or olive oil are best)
½ of a 7 ounce container plain Greek yogurt
2 tablespoons curry powder
1 teaspoon yellow mustard (just eyeball it, no need to measure)
1/2 cup raisins
2 stalks chopped celery
1 small or 1/2 medium red onion, thinly sliced
Extra virgin olive oil (EVOO), sea salt and black pepper

Directions

1. Put a med-large pot of water on to boil with a large pinch of salt.
2. Cut scrubbed potatoes into bite-sized pieces (about ¾ inch square).
3. While water is coming to a boil, add yogurt, mayo, 1 tablespoon EVOO, mustard, curry powder, ¾ tsp salt and some black pepper in a large mixing bowl, stir together with a spoon.
4. When water boils, add potatoes and boil 7 minutes, then add green beans and boil 5 more minute until beans are bright green but still crisp and potatoes are tender.
5. Strain the beans and potatoes, add to the mixing bowl along with the chicken, raisins, chopped celery and sliced onion. Toss together and taste – add salt and pepper as needed.

COOK'S NOTES

Like many of my recipes this is simply a template. Use whatever vegetables, beans, nuts and grains you like and have on-hand.

CHICKPEAS, GREEN BEANS AND BROWN RICE WITH TAHINI DRESSING

Adapted from 101 Cookbooks
Total Prep Time: 45 minutes
Active Time: 25 minutes
Serves: 4

Ingredients
1 cup uncooked brown rice

3 cups cooked chickpeas, from 2 cans or 1 cup dried

1 onion, minced

½ lb green beans, can be fresh or frozen, cut into 1-2 inch pieces

½ cup toasted almonds, chopped or slivered

3 tsp minced garlic, from about 3 cloves

¼ cup tahini (sesame seed paste)

1 lemon

Extra virgin olive oil (EVOO), sea salt, freshly cracked black pepper

Directions
1. Prepare the rice per package instructions (for most brown rice simmer the rice in 2 cups of water in a covered pan for 45 minutes).

2. Prepare the dressing: whisk together the tahini, juice and zest of the lemon, 1 tsp garlic, 2 tablespoons of EVOO, 2 tablespoons of hot water, and ½ tsp salt. Set aside.

3. When the rice is nearly done (about 10 minutes left) prepare the vegetables: place a large sauté pan over medium heat and add a large drizzle of EVOO. Add the onion and sauté for 3 minutes until fragrant, then add the chickpeas, green beans, and remaining garlic and sauté for another 3-5 minutes until the beans have turned bright green and the chickpeas are warm. If the green beans need a little boost, add a few tablespoons of water to the pan then cover it – the steam will quickly cook the beans in a minute or two.

4. Add the brown rice, almonds, and dressing to the pan and toss everything to combine.

COOK'S 🥕 **NOTES**

GINGER SHRIMP, SNAP PEA AND RED PEPPER STIR FRY WITH BROWN RICE

Total Prep Time: 30 minutes
Active Time: 20 minutes
Serves: 4

Ingredients

1 lb domestic uncooked shrimp, deveined and peeled, thawed (can sub
(meat alternative such as extra-firm tofu or seitan)

2 tablespoons grated fresh ginger root (from about 2 inches) or sub jarred minced

1 lb sugar snap peas, washed (trim off ends/pull off strings if you want*)

½ bag or 1 cup frozen corn (or 2 cobs fresh, cut from cob)

1 red bell pepper, washed and diced

½ small red onion, diced

3 cloves garlic, diced

Lime, for garnish

1 cup uncooked brown rice, rinsed

Extra virgin olive oil (EVOO), sea salt, freshly cracked black pepper

Directions

1. Bring approximately 6 cups of water in a medium-large pot to boil. Rinse rice in a fine sieve. When water is boiling, add rice to pot, reduce heat to simmer and put on the lid. Set timer for 45 minutes. Strain in a fine-mesh sieve when the rice is done cooking and let the steam escape for several minutes.

2. About 20 minutes before the rice will be done start preparing the stir-fry. Pat shrimp dry if necessary, and toss in a bowl with a tablespoon of olive oil, a teaspoon of the minced garlic, tablespoon of the minced ginger, a pinch of salt, and a pinch of crushed red pepper.

3. In a large skillet, heat up another tablespoon or two of the olive oil over medium heat, and sauté the onion, red pepper, and snap peas until the vegetables are tender but still crisp (about 5 minutes). The peas should be bright green. Add the corn and the rest of the garlic and ginger and sauté another minute, until the garlic is fragrant and the corn is thawed.

COOK'S NOTES

4) Push the vegetables to the outside of the pan and add the shrimp. Sauté until the shrimp has turned pink and curls (time depends on the size of the shrimp, but this happens quite fast – usually in 1-3 minutes). Turn off heat.

5) Stir vegetables and shrimp together to combine flavors. Season with additional salt and pepper to taste and serve over the rice, with lime wedges.

COOK'S   NOTES

EGGPLANT AND ZUCCHINI PARMESAN

Total Prep Time: 45 minutes
Active Time: 30 minutes
Serves: 4

Ingredients

2 medium eggplants, cut length-wise into ¼ inch thick slices
1 medium zucchini, cut length-wise into ¼ inch thick slices
1 1/2-2 cups Fresh Tomato Sauce
1 cup grated parmesan or pecorino romano cheese
3 cups grated mozzarella cheese
Optional: 1 cup fresh basil or 2 tsp dried Italian herbs (oregano, basil, etc)
Extra virgin olive oil (EVOO), sea salt, freshly cracked black pepper

Directions

1. Pre-heat your oven to 375 degrees, or pre-heat your grill
2. Brush the eggplant and zucchini strips with a little EVOO and sprinkle with salt and pepper. Either roast single-layer in your oven for 8-10 minutes per side, until soft and lightly toasted, or grill for 3-4 minutes per side. Set aside.
3. Use a 13 x 9 inch pan or similarly sized casserole dish. Spread about 2/3 cup of tomato sauce in the bottom of the dish. Top with 1 layer of eggplant, then 1 cup of mozzarella cheese, then 1/3 cup of parmesan cheese, then some herbs, if using.
4. Repeat the layers, this time with sauce, then zucchini, cheeses and herbs. Finish with a final layer of sauce, eggplant, cheeses and herbs.
5. Bake uncovered for 30-35 minutes until the casserole is bubbling and the cheese has melted. If you can, allow the casserole to cool for 10-15 minutes before slicing and serving.

COOK'S NOTES

SAUTÉED COD WITH TARRAGON LEMON BUTTER, LENTILS AND SPINACH

Adapted from Sautéed Cod with Lentils, Gourmet 2004
Total Prep Time: 35 minutes
Active Time: 20 minutes
Serves: 4

Ingredients

1 cup dried lentils

3 tablespoons butter, grass-fed is best

1 onion, minced

2 teaspoons minced garlic, from about 3 cloves

¼ cup chopped fresh tarragon

3 tablespoons lemon juice and 1 tsp zest, from 1 lemon

8 ounces frozen chopped spinach or sub fresh

½ tsp whole seed or Dijon mustard

4 5-ounce cod filets

Extra virgin olive oil (EVOO), sea salt, freshly cracked black pepper

Directions

1. Bring 3 cups of lightly salted water to boil in a small saucepan with a tight fitting lid. Rinse the lentils in cold water then add them to the boiling water. Reduce the heat to a simmer, then cover and cook until the lentils are tender, about 20 minutes, then drain and place in a large mixing bowl.

2. Meanwhile, put a large sauté pan over medium heat along with one tablespoon of butter. Add the minced onion and sauté until softened, about 3 minutes. Add the garlic and spinach and sauté another 3-4 minutes until thawed or wilted. Place this mixture in the mixing bowl with the lentils, along with half of the lemon juice, half of the tarragon, the lemon zest and a small drizzle of EVOO. Toss everything together and adjust salt and pepper to taste.

3. Drizzle a little EVOO in the sauté pan and add one tablespoon of butter. Sprinkle the fish lightly with salt and pepper then add it to the sauté pan. Sauté for about 2 minutes on one side, then flip and cook for approximately 2-3 minutes on the second side. Add half of the tarragon, the mustard, the other half of the lemon juice, another tablespoon of butter and some fresh black pepper to the pan. Let everything cook together and coat the fish for one minute. Turn off the heat. Serve the fish over-top of the lentils.

COOK'S NOTES ─────────────────────────────────

KASHA WITH MUSHROOMS, KALE AND A FRIED EGG

Total Prep Time: 30 minutes
Active Time: 30 minutes
Serves: 4

Ingredients

1 ½ cups dried kasha (roasted buckwheat groats)

1 cup apple cider or apple juice, or sub water

1 onion, sliced thinly

8 ounces sliced mushrooms

1 bunch kale rinsed, de-stemmed, and roughly chopped

1 teaspoon apple cider vinegar

2 teaspoons minced garlic, from about 2 cloves

4 eggs, preferably pasture-raised

For garnish: soy sauce or coconut aminos,

Extra virgin olive oil (EVOO), sea salt and black pepper

Directions

1. In a small-medium soup pot with a tight-fitting lid, bring the apple cider plus 1 ½ cups of water to a boil along with a pinch of salt. Add the kasha, cover, reduce to a simmer and cook for 15 minutes.

2. Meanwhile, add a tablespoon of EVOO to a large sauté pan (one that does have a lid) over medium heat. Add the mushrooms and sauté until they let off their juices and are sweet, about 7 minutes, seasoning them with a little salt and pepper along the way.

3. Add the sliced onion to the pan and sauté until tender, about 3 minutes. Then add the kale and garlic and stir to combine all ingredients. Pour about ¼ cup of water in the pan and then place the lid on top, to allow the kale to steam. Steam for about 3 minutes, then remove the lid and sprinkle the mixture with some salt and pepper, to taste.

4. Place servings of kasha in individual serving bowls, topped by the kale and mushroom mixture. In a little EVOO, fry four eggs (you can do this in the same pan that the kale mixture was in) to top each bowl with, with yolks cooked how you like them. If you like, drizzle with a little soy sauce and serve.

COOK'S NOTES

This is one of my husband's favorites, and it's better than take-out. Look for soba noodles in the international aisle, which usually come in either a buckwheat/wheat combination, or 100% buckwheat.

BEEF AND BROCCOLI WITH SOBA NOODLES

Total Prep Time: 30 minutes
Active Time: 15 minutes
Serves: 4

Ingredients
2 tsp toasted sesame oil
1- inch piece fresh ginger, grated
4 teaspoons minced garlic, from about 4 cloves
1 large onion, sliced
1 lb flank steak, sliced into ½ inch thick slices (cut across the grain)
4 cups of broccoli florets – can use 1-lb package frozen or 1 head
2 carrots, grated
3 tablespoons soy sauce or coconut aminos
2 tablespoons of honey
1 tablespoon oyster sauce
1 teaspoon chili paste
1 tablespoon corn starch
1 package soba noodles (buckwheat noodles)
Extra virgin olive oil (EVOO), sea salt, freshly cracked black pepper

Directions
1. Cook soba noodles per package instructions.
2. Whisk together the soy sauce, honey, oyster sauce, chili paste and cornstarch in a small bowl until lumps are gone. Set aside.
3. Heat a drizzle of EVOO in a large sauté pan over medium heat. Sauté onion for 3 minutes, then add broccoli for another 5 minutes until the broccoli is bright green and tender.

COOK'S NOTES

4. While veggies are sautéing, peel carrots (or just give them a good scrub) and grate with a box grater in the larger round holes. Add the garlic, ginger and carrots and sauté another minute until fragrant

5. Push veggies to the side of the pan and add the beef. Sauté until beef is cooked to just below your desired doneness, about 3-5 minutes. Add the sauce to the pan and bring to a simmer, stirring in the beef and veggies, until the sauce thickens, about 2-3 minutes. Serve the beef and vegetables over the soba noodles.

COOK'S NOTES

This casserole is as beautiful as it is tasty and nourishing, with vibrant greens and orange. If you'd like a fully vegan dish you can omit the cheese.

BUTTERCUP SQUASH AND SPINACH LASAGNA

Total Prep Time: 1 hour and 30 minutes
Active Time: 45 minutes
Serves: 4

Ingredients

12 large lasagna noodles, preferably whole grain, gluten-free noodles are fine

1 large winter squash (buttercup, butternut, etc), peel and seeds removed, then cut roughly into 1-inch cubes – this will be about 5 cups of cut squash

1 lb package frozen chopped spinach, or 16 ounces fresh

1 onion, minced

3 teaspoons minced garlic from about 3 cloves

6 ounces high-quality cheddar cheese, hormone-free, shredded

2 ounces grated parmesan or pecorino romano cheese, about ½ cup

16 ounces sliced mushrooms OR 12 ounces of chicken sausage

Extra virgin olive oil (EVOO), sea salt and black pepper

Directions

1. Steam the squash by placing about 1/2 -inch of water in a medium pot with a tight-fitting lid. Place the squash in the pot, bring the water to a simmer, cover and let cook for about 15 minutes until the squash is very tender when pierced with a sharp knife. Mash the squash with potato-masher and season with about ½ tsp of salt and some freshly ground black pepper.

2. Meanwhile cook the lasagna noodles per package instructions to al dente. If using gluten-free, under-cook the noodles by about 1/3 of the time.

3. While the squash and noodles are cooking prepare the spinach: place a drizzle of EVOO in a large sauté pan over medium heat. Add the onion and sauté until tender, about 3 minutes, then add the garlic and sauté another minute. Add the spinach and cook until frozen spinach has thawed and most of the moisture has evaporated, or until fresh spinach has wilted. Season the spinach with some salt and pepper to taste..

COOK'S ✿ NOTES

4. Move the spinach to a bowl and sauté the mushrooms or chicken sausage until the mushrooms release their moisture, or the chicken sausage is cooked through. Season the mushrooms with a little salt and pepper.

5. Grease a 13 x 9 casserole dish with a little EVOO. Place a layer of lasagna noodles in the bottom of the pan – you should use about 4 of them. Top with 1/3 of the squash, ½ of the spinach mixture, ½ of the mushrooms or sausage, and 1/3 of the cheeses. Repeat the layers, ending with the final layer of noodles topped only with squash and cheese.

6. Bake the lasagna at 375 degrees, covered for 30 minutes then uncovered for another 15 minutes.

COOK'S NOTES

WHITE BEAN AND TURKEY CHILI WITH SWEET POTATOES AND JALAPENO

Total Prep Time: 45 minutes
Active Time: 30 minutes
Serves: 4

Ingredients

4 ½ cups cooked white beans, such as cannellini, from 1 ½ cups dried or 3 cans

1 lb ground turkey, preferably free-range and pasture-fed

1 jalapeno minced small, seeds removed if you want less spice

2 poblano or green bell peppers, minced (use bell peppers if you want less spice)

4 teaspoons minced garlic, from about 4 cloves

3 teaspoons ground cumin

1 ½ teaspoons ground coriander

1 teaspoon chili powder

4 cups chicken or turkey stock

2 cups chopped tomatoes, from about 1 can

1 onion, minced or chopped small

1 large sweet potato or yam, scrubbed and cut into ½ inch dice

Optional: sour cream, plain Greek yogurt, and/or cheddar cheese for topping

Extra virgin olive oil (EVOO), sea salt, freshly cracked black pepper

Directions

1. Heat a large soup pot or Dutch oven over medium heat. Add some EVOO and the ground turkey and sauté, breaking up the turkey into bite-sized pieces until the turkey is mostly cooked through, about 5 minutes. Season with a little salt and pepper while cooking.

2. Remove the turkey to a small bowl or plate. Add the minced onions, peppers, and spices and sauté until the vegetables are soft and the spices are fragrant, about 4 minutes.

3. Add the stock, tomatoes, browned turkey (including any juices in the bowl), and beans and bring to a simmer. Simmer for about 10 minutes, then add the sweet potatoes and simmer for an additional 10 minutes, just until the sweet potatoes are tender – you won't want to cook them too long or they will become mushy and dissolve. Taste the chili and season with salt and pepper before serving.

4. Serve with a dollop of sour cream or plain yogurt and a little grated cheddar cheese.

COOK'S NOTES

HEARTY KALE AND WHITE BEAN SOUP

Total Prep Time: 35 minutes
Active Time: 20 minutes
Serves: 4

Ingredients

1 bunch kale, ribs removed and roughly chopped

1 medium onion, diced

2 carrots, peeled and sliced into half moons

1 russet or sweet potato, cut into ¾ inch cubes

6-8 ounces ham steak or kielbasa, cubed (can omit or add an additional cup of beans or sautéed mushrooms)

3 cups cooked white beans, from 2 cans or 1 cup dried

4 teaspoons minced garlic, from about 4 cloves

4 cups water or stock (chicken or vegetable)

2 cups chopped tomatoes

1 tsp cumin

Grated parmesan or pecorino romano cheese, for topping

Extra virgin olive oil (EVOO), sea salt, freshly cracked black pepper

Directions

1. Place a large stock pot over medium heat and add a large drizzle of EVOO

2. Sauté the onions and carrots and cook for 4 minutes until softened. Add the garlic and sauté for another minute until fragrant.

3. Add the remaining ingredients and bring to a simmer. Cover and simmer for about 15 minutes until the vegetables are tender.

4. Season with sea salt and pepper and serve topped with grated parmesan or pecorino romano.

COOK'S NOTES

-5-
IT'S YOUR JOURNEY

Rock the Boat, Don't Tip It Over

We are all somewhere on a spectrum between where we were and where we want to be. Food habits are deeply ingrained and the changes you're making are part of a journey. I encourage you to enjoy the process of exploring new foods; you don't have to be "there," at your ideal goal, tomorrow or the next day. Extreme changes in a short period of time, which some fad diets recommend, can stress your body and mind and actually make the pendulum swing back farther in the opposite direction. I experienced this myself when I attempted the South Beach and Atkins diets back in the early 2000s. I spent the following six months fantasizing and indulging in carbs that I never would have eaten before the diets. (Hello, HoHos).

I encourage you to make changes gradually but consistently at a pace that is somewhere in the zone of challenging but still comfortable. Focus on your progress, not anyone else's, and find what works for you.

Grow Your Food-Body-Mood Connection

All foods make us feel a certain way, and the results are very individualized. The more attention you pay to how certain foods make you feel, the better you'll be able to eat strategically. Food becomes a tool in your toolbox. Some people feel great eating whole grain cereals at breakfast, others feel their best eating mostly proteins and fats like eggs and avocados. Some people are strongly negatively affected by caffeine, others are pretty immune to it. Allergies and sensitivities are highly individualized. Pay attention and see what foods make you feel good, because over time you'll internalize that information and you'll automatically begin to choose foods that affect you positively.

Most importantly, be kind with yourself along the way. If your goal is to reduce sugar, and you cave in one day and eat some birthday cake, it's OK. Relax. As an analytical person I often tell my clients that there are no "mistakes," there's only data collection. Make a mental note of how it made you feel and move on.

I've been eating gluten-free for nearly five years now because I feel so much better this way. However, along the way I've indulged many times. Each time there's a consequence. The more consequences I experience, the less attractive those cheat foods become for me. The acknowledgment of the consequence is conscious, but the way it affects my decision-making moving forward is more subconscious; those foods have simply become less desirable. Over time the same will happen for you; you'll begin to choose foods based not only on how they taste, but also on how they make you feel, and the ability to make good decisions will get easier and easier.

Get Help if You Need It

Our society glorifies individual perseverance, which is important, but support and a fresh perspective go a long way. If you need support, or are making all of the changes you think you should be making and still aren't seeing the results you want, it's time for some help.

Working with a certified health coach can help you prioritize, identify patterns that you're stuck in, diagnose food intolerances, support you in whatever else will help you the most, and most importantly make the process fun and enjoyable. More information about health coaching is available at www.eathappynow.com, and you can email me directly at alissa@eathappynow.com.

———————————— Allison's Story ————————————

Allison was a professional in her early thirties when we began working together. Much like me when I was in my twenties, and before I changed my ways of eating, Allison was technically healthy, yet something felt off. She ate a convenience-oriented diet, not of fast-food, but of grocery-store purchased processed foods with minimal variety. When we began working together she felt flat and uninspired. Allison's own words are written below, and are a testimonial to the vitality that fresh unprocessed foods can bring to your body and mind:

"Working with Alissa revolutionized the way I take care of myself on a daily basis. When I first started working with Alissa, I wasn't sick, I just didn't feel 'well.' I had some back and neck pain, my stomach would sometimes get thrown off, and my energy would wane. I tended to be impatient when it came to eating and didn't plan ahead, so I didn't cook anything that took longer than 5 minutes. I also worried about consuming enough vitamins and minerals.

That feels like a long time ago, because my life is so different now. Working with Alissa led me to think more deeply about the role food plays in my life. Now, I make a concerted effort to read labels and to buy local or organic fruits, vegetables and grains because I know it makes me feel good. After cooking with and eating fresh, local ingredients, I feel a lightness and a happiness I never knew could come from food before. Together we formed an integrative approach that works for me, because I have permission to 'be bad' sometimes. But, I'm so enthusiastic for the new healthier foods that I'm their biggest cheerleader around my friends and colleagues.

Working with Alissa was a pleasure. Each time we met, the sessions felt tailored to where I was in the process, and I left each one with renewed energy and excitement. Alissa generously offered advice, and often, new foods or recipes to try that are now staples in my diet. She is extremely knowledgeable and provided great information about all of my questions. She listened compassionately when we talked about all the other stressors in my life and supported me at each milestone I made. My goals were her goals, and she helped me reach them. Thanks to Alissa, I'm not just healthier, I feel happier, too."

-6-
RESOURCES

Resources

Eathappynow.com

Information on health coaching, whole foods meal plans and recipes, and speaking engagements

Eatwild.com

Find naturally-raised meats and animal products near you and a wealth of information on natural foods

Localharvest.org

Locate farmer's markets, community-supported agriculture programs (CSAs), and other local food information

Ewg.org

The Environmental Working Group provides valuable information on how to eat foods clean of pesticides and chemicals as well as other environmental issues

Cspinet.org

The Center for Science in the Public Interest provides science-based research and recommendations on food additives as well as other nutrition and food safety issues.

Made in the USA
Charleston, SC
17 November 2014